# ANIMAL CRACKERS

## IRISH PET STORIES

### COLM KEANE & UNA O'HAGAN

CAPEL
ISLAND

Copyright Colm Keane & Una O'Hagan 2016

First published in Ireland in 2016

by

CAPEL ISLAND PRESS
Baile na nGall,
Ring, Dungarvan,
County Waterford,
Ireland

ISBN 978-0-9559133-7-2

Printed and bound by Clays Ltd, St Ives plc
Typesetting and cover design by Typeform Ltd

For Seán

Colm Keane has published 25 books, including six number one bestsellers, among them *Going Home*, *We'll Meet Again* and *Heading for the Light*. He is a graduate of Trinity College, Dublin, and Georgetown University, Washington DC. As a broadcaster, he won a Jacob's Award and a Glaxo Fellowship for European Science Writers.

Una O'Hagan is a newsreader with Radio Telefís Éireann. A DIT graduate in journalism, she has interviewed Nelson Mandela, accompanied President Mary Robinson on a 1992 state visit to Australia and hosted live programmes on the deaths of former Taoisigh Jack Lynch and Garret FitzGerald and the state visit of Queen Elizabeth II to Ireland.

# CONTENTS

A black cat crossing your path signifies that the animal is going somewhere.

Groucho Marx (1890 – 1977)

# INTRODUCTION

Dogs look up to us, cats look down on us and pigs treat us as equals. It was former British Prime Minister Sir Winston Churchill who said that. The astuteness of his remark is evident in the real-life stories about Ireland's favourite animals and pets contained in this book.

Often hilarious, frequently uplifting, sometimes heroic and at times extraordinary tales are featured not only of cats, dogs and pigs but of other animals including horses, donkeys, rabbits, parrots, hamsters and lots more furry friends.

One thing all these animals have in common is the warmth and comfort, happiness and joy, loyalty and devotion they have brought to those who have known and loved them over the years. To many, they are God's greatest gift.

We have had a bit of experience on that front ourselves. We may not own a dog at present, but a Labrador definitely owns us. He turned up one morning at our gate, shortly after eight o'clock, barking loudly and looking to be taken for a walk. He has done the same thing every day since, and we have become the best of friends. He probably thinks he is doing us a favour, but we know better.

His name is Frankie – a gold-coloured Labrador, aged 11, somewhat overweight and with the most affable personality you could imagine. Somewhere along the way, about two years ago, we gave him a first taste of San Pellegrino sparkling water. He now drinks four bottles a day – the first at the gate in the morning, the rest during our walks. He is a costly dog!

1

His other weakness is food. He will eat anything. When the hunger hits him, he leads us to a shop nearby knowing they sell sausages and sausage rolls. He waits outside the door and barks if we take too long. He always thanks us, nudging us with his nose as a gesture of gratitude.

Frankie belongs to our neighbours, the Currans, who treat him like a king. With us, he lives a second existence, walking, swimming, chasing rocks, playing football, meeting other dogs and, when the weather is good, joining us outside our house for a snooze.

He has a passion for the sea. He loves it. He would play in it all day if he could. He often stares out to the distant horizon, lost in thought. Those intense moments are special, drawn no doubt from his breed's original role as helpers for the fishermen working in the seas around Newfoundland.

Frankie really is one big ball of love and affection and a joy to be with. He knows no malice, holds no grudges and never lets us down. To paraphrase the English novelist George Eliot, he is always agreeable, asks no questions and passes no criticisms. He is loyal, considerate and kind. He barks occasionally, but that's only to hurry us up. He really is a wonder dog.

Many animals like Frankie exist around the country. Most are household pets, others work for their keep, more provide support to people with special needs. Although sometimes their value is overlooked, they provide company for the lonely, are models of compassion and create indelible bonds with their human companions.

They love to play, eat, be noticed and explore. They are most grateful for the smallest of gestures and acts of kindness. Like us, they get bored, feel pain and suffer loss. As parents, they care deeply for their offspring, nurturing them, watching over them and smothering them with love and affection. They live for neither the past nor future but concentrate on the present, something we humans could productively replicate in our lives.

One day, Frankie will no longer be with us; he is, after all, getting old. In the meantime, we treasure his friendship and cherish his company. But Frankie is not alone; indeed, there are many animals like him in the pages ahead. Read on, take your pick and enjoy the stories. They will warm your heart.

*Colm Keane & Una O'Hagan*

# MADCAP MARVELS

Irish mythical animal stories are eccentric, to say the least. Take Cú Chulainn, for instance. As a boy, he killed a guard dog owned by a man named Culann. He promised to protect the man's house until a replacement dog was found. He became known as Cú Chulainn, or the 'Hound of Culann', as a result.

There are many other oddball examples. The Children of Lir were magically turned into swans. The Salmon of Knowledge possessed all the world's wisdom. The phantom queen, Morrigan, appeared as a crow. Bran and Sceolan were hounds of human descent.

The animals featured in the stories that follow may not be quite so bizarre or exaggerated. As you will see, however, their tales are no less remarkable than those from Ireland's mythical past.

M. C. HARDCASTLE describes his drake, Hannibal Heyes, who believes he is human and not just a pet.

I got Hannibal Heyes at a mart near Enniskillen. It was a frosty day and I was heading for home. I spotted this little drake or duck in a cage. He was only a tiny baby and coloured black, although he developed other colours later on including a darkish green. He was on his own, the only one that was left, and he looked so cute.

I paid four euro for him and he was happy to get out of the cage. The man I bought him from gave me a shoebox and punched holes in it for air. I didn't want him suffocating on the way home, about an hour away. He fitted into the shoebox, in one corner, the lid went down, and that was it.

I brought him home and I walked around the house with him in my jacket pocket. My wife didn't even realise he was there for at least half an hour. I was walking around the kitchen and she didn't notice. 'What's that sticking up?' she suddenly asked. 'Ah, that's a little duck I got!' I said. It was only afterwards I discovered it was a drake.

I decided to christen him Hannibal Heyes. The name came from the television series *Alias Smith and Jones* from the 1970s. Instead of going to dances, I spent a lot of my time watching television when I was young. I loved the old westerns and detective programmes and stuff like that. I thought Hannibal Heyes was catchy and it has stuck to him ever since.

He always responds to the name now when I call him. For example, I will stand at the garage door, on a wet day, and he will be a long way down from me and I will shout, 'Heyes, come on, it's raining! You shouldn't be out in the rain!' and he'll come running up.

After a while, I built him his own house with his own name written over the door. He has everything in it but Sky TV. It's a wooden structure, about eight feet by four feet, and it belongs to him only. It wouldn't do if any of the cats went in. There would be a bit of a dust-up. He's very protective of his own department. He eats there and sleeps there unless he's sick.

It wasn't long before Heyes didn't see himself as being a drake at all. You would notice him having a look at himself in a mirror I have in the garage. He'd walk straight in and have a look. He would also come and visit us in the house. Sometimes, he wouldn't fancy the people who might be visiting. He would come running in, racing around, ducking under tables and chairs, looking about as if to say, 'What are you doing here?' Then he'd walk out.

He would also watch videos with me. I remember watching *McCloud* one night. It's a police drama with Dennis Weaver. Heyes was sitting alongside me, with my arm around him. In this particular episode, McCloud was sent out to rescue an animal which was causing havoc over in Manhattan. It turned out to be a duck. Heyes happened to notice the duck and he leapt straight out of the chair, went across the floor and stared up at the television. He knew it was part of his family. It was really funny.

Another time, I was watching *The Boys of Twilight*, featuring two lawmen. In this episode, they were trying to find a bunch of ducks and drakes. They decided to use a duck to see if they could flush out where the rest of the ducks had gone. The duck walked down the street, lawmen and all, straight into this store where they thought the animals might be. And Heyes was watching that! Man, if you could have seen the eyes on him!

There are people he doesn't like. There's one particular man who comes to visit me and Heyes took a dislike to him. That man lost the leg of his trousers here one day. Heyes chased him and the man got frightened. He caught himself going across the gate. When I got there, the leg of the trousers was on the ground. It was a disaster. When that man comes to visit now, he rings me up to make sure Heyes is locked in before he comes. He won't visit otherwise.

Heyes really rules the place. There was one incident where a small kitten arrived after being slung out on the road outside.

The bigger cats didn't take too kindly to its arrival. They got around it and started aggravating it, stressing it out a bit. But Heyes came plodding over, just like some sort of lord, got in between the cats and started pecking them. He got them out of the way so that the kitten could escape. Heyes then stood upright and started flapping his wings, which he does when he's very proud of himself. The kitten is here to this day.

He had an awful accident once, when he was 12. He has a fondness of following me around, and this particular day he followed me into the garage. It was a bad, windy, wet morning. He was just behind me and didn't I close the door and catch his foot! I knew the leg was badly damaged. I knew he was in trouble.

I brought him in to see the vet. Had the break been further up, the vet could have fixed it using lollipop sticks. Instead, he had to anaesthetise Heyes, use a drill, bore a hole each side of the break, and put some pins in. Had the bone shattered at any time during this procedure, Hannibal Heyes would be gone. The operation worked. That vet is a genius.

Heyes, as we talk, is 14 years old and in top-class health. He has been a great friend to me and great company. My wife used to do home help and I'd be here on my own, but he'd be with me. The first thing I do every morning is go out to see how he is. No matter what's going on, I have to see him. Even when I'm away, I ring home to see how he is doing. I don't know what I'd do if anything happened to him. I'd never get over it.

You could almost say he is nearly human. He has the mind of a human, even if he can't write or read or things like that. I can honestly say that, for a drake, he's the next best thing to a human that I have ever seen. But he doesn't see it that way. I really think he doesn't know what he is – a drake. He thinks he's top cat, and I'd safely say he's not far wrong!

**MAY HICKEY's dog Bell was a big fan of Waterford hurler Dan Shanahan, especially at the height of his and his team's success in the first decade of this century.**

The Waterford hurlers were doing remarkably well at the time. Everyone was hyped up. Dan Shanahan would always be on the television playing in matches. After the dinner, I'd put on the television. Bell would sit on the back of the armchair to watch. She'd have her blue-and-white plait around her neck. She might have another plait under her stomach, tied with a little bow on top of her back.

Every time the commentator mentioned Dan Shanahan, Bell would go mad. He'd be saying, 'And it's Dan Shanahan again.....' and she'd be going nuts. You wouldn't believe it. I'd be saying, 'Bell! Bell! Calm down!' She'd be barking for the whole 70 minutes of the match, but when Dan would score a goal I'd shout and she'd start barking mad.

It got so bad that she'd eventually go crazy every time the name Dan Shanahan was mentioned. We'd have to spell out his name, D-a-n S-h-a-n-a-h-a-n, so that she wouldn't start barking. She was unbelievable. But Dan is a grand person. When I was working, I used to do up the window for the hurling and put up a big sign, 'There's no man like our Dan!'

I was in Dungarvan with her, one day, and who did I bump into but Dan. His mother is a cousin of my husband's, so I knew him. I said, 'Dan! I have your biggest fan in the world over in the car. Would you come over and say hello to her?' I'm sure he thought it was some girl or somebody, so we went over.

Who was there but my woman sitting in the car, looking out at Dan! I said, 'Do you want to give Dan shakehandsies now?' He got his little shakehands from Bell. I think he was amazed!

Bell was the dog that people didn't want. The people who owned her – who she had strayed into – rang their local radio station in Tipperary and said they were going away on holidays and they needed a home for the dog. My daughter took her. She knew that her sister was looking for a small dog, so she arrived with Bell in a box.

She was a little Jack Russell, coloured white with black and brown. From then on, she was with me the whole time. The minute I'd get out of bed, she'd know we were going somewhere and she'd stand on duty at the door. She'd sit on the mat and wouldn't budge. I'd say, 'Do you want to go?' And she'd be into the car like a bullet.

We'd go everywhere together, up the mountains and all. I'd make a flask of tea; she loved the tea. I'd make a sandwich for her, as well. I'd always tell her where we were going. I might say, 'We're going to Cork today' or 'We're going to Waterford today,' and she appreciated that.

She'd come with me to work and I'd be chatting away to her in the car. While I was at work, I'd keep her in the car across the road. I'd take her out and bring her for walks during the day and feed her. Everything she ate was what I was having. Even when I was laid up in bed with a broken leg, she spent the whole time lying there beside me. She was the most loyal, affectionate dog that anyone ever had.

She loved children. When our eldest granddaughter Millie would come to visit, she might be below in bed sick and Bell would go down and sit and mind her. You wouldn't believe it.

My son was here, one night, when Millie was only about three or four months old, and he was messing in front of the fire. He lifted Millie up in the air and caught her. Bell went for him because she was afraid he was at the child. She loved Millie.

Bell wasn't well for a while and I brought her to the vet. He said, 'She's old and it would be a kind thing to put her down.' I said, 'God! I couldn't do that!' I put her in my bed and made her nice and comfy. She looked very sad.

One day, we were sitting there looking at *Home and Away* and she sat up in the bed and started heaving like she wanted to get sick. I held her up and I said, 'It's alright, Bell.' But she haemorrhaged and she was gone in seconds. She was 14 and a half when she died.

Bell died on 28 August 2013. I was devastated. I wrapped her up in a blanket and a friend made a lovely little box. I have a little grave for her out in the back. There are little mounts and white stones all around the grave. I also say a prayer for her every night. But I don't have any Waterford things on her grave, although she loved the team.

There might never be a period similar to that again for the Waterford hurlers. Believe it or not, I was at the last All-Ireland we won, in 1959, when I was three years old. I was brought there by my mam and dad. I have loved Waterford ever since. I still am Waterford through and through, and my children are loyal Waterford, too.

My husband is from Tipperary. My son is married to a Cork woman, my daughter is married to a Cork man, and my other daughter is getting married to a Cork man. Even though Bell was originally from Tipperary, just like my husband, she was loyal to Waterford. There was no bigger fan of that team than

Bell. Nor was there any bigger fan of Dan Shanahan, whose likes we will never see again.

**PATRICIA ROCHE has had a lifelong love affair with pet rabbits.**

About 30 years ago, I was asked to look after a rabbit called Abigail. She was grey and lovely and fluffy. I really loved the look of her. She walked like a little pig and loved running on the grass. I was mesmerised by her. She came and never went home. That was the beginning of my love affair with my darling bunnies.

My next rabbit was Mrs. Beehive. Her hair was exactly like a beehive hairstyle from the 1960s, a bit like Dusty Springfield. Unfortunately, she loved to dig. She was a master digger. She eventually dug her way out and a fox got her. I made a vow that day that I would never, ever let another rabbit be taken by a fox.

Roger was one of my next rabbits, but his downfall was that he loved sweets. One day, my stepson left a tin of biscuits open and Roger took a bite out of every single biscuit. He tried them all – ginger nuts and custard creams, the lot. I even used to bake cakes for him. Roger would stand by the oven, waiting for the cakes to come out so he could have a slice of one of them. He got a bit obese, I'm afraid.

He also took a shine to the baby carrier. He looked at it and decided, 'This is the perfect home for me!' So he got in. He also used to pull the socks off the baby's feet. He thought it was hilarious. There's a story every day with rabbits.

He ran away one day. We were laughing about him, but I can't remember why. Rabbits don't like you laughing about them. He got really furious. He ran down the garden and got into the next garden at the back. It was full of nettles and briars. He would not come out. We eventually had to lift him out. We brought him home and he was a bit embarrassed.

We got a female, Peggy Sue, to keep him company. She was beautiful. As soon as Roger saw her, he absolutely fell in love with her. He idolised the ground she walked on. They used to sit together like companions. He was just so nice. He was the love of my life, my boy. After he died, we decided to get more. We've had J. R. and Rowley, Bea and Bo-bo, Cheeko and Pawdy ever since.

J. R. became our alarm clock. He would come up to the bedroom every morning at about ten minutes to six. For rabbits, stamping the back legs is a sign of danger, so he'd stamp up the stairs. The noise would be very loud because the back legs are very strong. Then he'd start stamping on the floor up in the bedroom, telling us it's time to get up. He'd then jump up on the bed and tickle us with his little whiskers, so we had to get up.

He understood weekends, when he would never disturb you until about eight o'clock. But Bank Holidays really threw him. If there was a Monday Bank Holiday, he couldn't understand it. He'd be frantically trying to tell you, 'You're going to be late for work!'

One particular night, at about quarter past one, he woke us up while stamping up the stairs. He got into the bed and got under the bottom sheet. He started stamping on the mattress. It was really loud. There was no way he would let us sleep. We thought somebody might have broken in, but none of us went down. We were too scared.

In the morning, the penny dropped. I went into the sitting-room. My little step-granddaughter had been visiting us and she had one of those little helium balloons. It had been up on the ceiling and had fallen down. There it was on the floor. J. R. must have thought that somebody had just dropped in from outer space!

There is another story, this one concerning Bea. She had some bunnies one time. I remember it was a very cold winter, which went on and on and on. I came home from work one day and I had a scarf around my neck. I left it down on the chair. When I went to hang it up, I couldn't find it. I thought I must have left it on the train. But then I looked in the dark side of her hutch and she had all her little bunnies wrapped up in the scarf.

We had a mouse at one time, as well. When we saw him, we were scared there would be a million mice but there was only one. We tried to catch him but he always escaped. He then became quite brave and friendly. He would watch us and look at us. He became quite visible in the end and made himself at home.

He used to pull Bea's whiskers. She didn't like it at all. One day, she'd had enough. She jammed him up against the skirting board and bashed him with her paw. She wasn't taking any more nonsense. The poor little thing! He didn't pull her whiskers again, that's for sure!

Overall, I have had about 20 rabbits. The look of them, the feel of them, the softness of them, the innocence of them – all of those attributes stand out. They are non-aggressive unless provoked. They are good with children. You could leave babies with them; they wouldn't hurt them. They might give them a little scratch if they jumped on them, but that would be rare.

They have no vindictiveness in them. They look lovely with those furry little ears. The way they run and jump is so cute. Unfortunately, they have very short lives. That's the thing with rabbits – you have a lot of heartache. You see them grow and develop, and then they leave you. It can be hard to take. They are so loving and affectionate. When they go, you miss them so much.

**DES HALL recalls the story of a gun dog who understood when an order just wasn't fair.**

This story goes back to the time of the Second World War, when I was growing up. There was a man my father knew who liked bird shooting, but his big strength was in training gun dogs. He'd make a gun dog do anything, flushing out birds and also fetching them for you. He specialised in the training of Springer Spaniels.

In this particular instance, he had a litter of Springer Spaniels and he kept one of the pups. It was a small Springer, which he beautifully trained, and it had perfect manners. The dog's name was Brian. Whenever my father would go shooting with the dog's trainer, the man would say, 'Leave your dogs at home. I'll supply them.' He knew my father's dogs were nowhere near as reliable as his, and certainly nowhere near as reliable as Brian.

On one occasion, a nephew of the trainer came to stay and they decided to go down to the North Slob in Wexford to go shooting wildfowl and see if they might get a few geese. They took off during a spell of wicked cold weather. After they arrived, they ranged around for the best part of the day. It really was horribly cold, with ice everywhere. They picked up damn few ducks. They hadn't much of a day at all.

Towards evening, they got back to where the car was. They got out the sandwiches and hot coffee. They put Brian into a heavy sacking-bag, which they kept in the car. It tied up around Brian's neck, keeping him warm and the car clean. He snuggled down into his bag after the day's hunting.

They hadn't the first bite of the sandwich gone when the nephew said, 'Look! The geese are coming in!' He had always wanted to bag a goose, so he grabbed his gun and headed off up the slob. After a while, there was the sound of *bang! bang!* It was followed by the sound of a goose dropping. He said to his uncle, 'I've got a goose! I've got a goose! But it's at the far side of the big cut. Can I get Brian to fetch it?'

His uncle opened up the bag, but Brian wouldn't get out. He had to physically take him out and put the bag back in the car. The nephew said, 'Heel!' and headed off to the slob. But Brian didn't follow; instead, he headed back to the car and sat down. The nephew said again, 'Heel!' but Brian wouldn't move.

Brian was making a protest. He had been brought back after a day's work, been put into his cosy bag, and that was it. He was on strike. He clearly felt, 'This isn't fair. This isn't proper.' He felt offended.

The nephew had to drag him off to the slob. When they got there, the nephew ordered Brian into the cut but again Brian wouldn't budge. He had to pitch Brian into the cut, after which he swam off and headed to the far side. The dog hunted around the far bank and eventually found the goose. He brought it back to the bank on the far side and then he sat down.

'OK, boy, fetch it!' the nephew shouted out. Immediately, Brian started pulling off huge mouthfuls of feathers. He took off three huge mouthfuls and then stared back across the river.

The nephew said again, 'Fetch!' Two more mouthfuls of feathers were taken off. This happened again and again. Every time the nephew roared instructions at Brian, more mouthfuls of feathers would be prised off.

The nephew was a very hardy lad and determined to have his goose. Despite the weather, he took off his clothes down to his pelt. He went straight into the cut and went up the bank on the far side. There was the goose, as naked as he was, but there was no dog. All he could see was a naked goose and an awful lot of feathers. Knowing he was going to freeze, he grabbed the goose, went back into the cut, got out the far side, put his clothes on as fast as he could and headed back to the car.

When he arrived at the car, his uncle said, 'I wondered what had happened to you. Brian has been back here for the last five minutes.' The nephew explained what had happened. By the time he had finished, his uncle was shrieking with laughter. He opened the car and there was Brian in his nice cosy bag. He looked out at the nephew as if he had never met him before.

The way Brian had taken it out on the nephew was utterly beautiful. He had to think out what he was doing. This was the most superbly-trained dog; he couldn't do wrong, yet he plotted this. He must have been a brilliant dog. His intelligence was well beyond instinct. After a couple of sandwiches and a cup of hot coffee, the nephew started to see the fun of it and broke his heart laughing, too. He realised he had come second-best.

The uncle went on training dogs but has gone to his reward long since. Sadly, the nephew, who was a great lad and on leave from the British Army at the time of the event in Wexford, went back to the war and got killed by the Germans in North Africa. He's buried out there now. I also remember the dog, Brian, very well. He was exceptional. I always recall him as the dog with the perfect manners, a lovely dog and perfectly trained, but with a great ability to know when something wasn't fair.

**ZOE recounts the life story of an affable pet pig named Arnold.**

My dad grew up in a tiny little house, on a little road, in the countryside of County Kildare. There were only a few other houses around. He lived in the house with his dad and mom and brothers and sisters. His dad used to be a farmer and he looked after cows and sheep. He had his own farm, but he eventually couldn't afford to keep it so he worked for the people around him.

The family were always in contact with animals. They loved them and they would look after sheep and cows from the fields across the road. If a calf was born young or was sick, my nanny would bring it in and keep it warm at the range, and stuff like that. One animal they brought in that way was a little pig they named Arnold, which they decided to keep as a pet.

The pig was really small when the family first got him. My nanny used to feed him from a bottle and put him under the range to keep him warm. Because of that, he got used to the house and he would come in and walk around. If the weather was harsh, they'd keep him in the house for the night and he'd sleep on a newspaper. Otherwise, he would sleep outside, on his side, up against the back door.

When he would drop into the house, he'd watch as my nanny cooked the dinner and he listened to everything she said. He would sit there, looking at her, and she would talk to him. She might say, 'Come on over here, Arnold,' and he would stand up and trot over. She might give him something to eat from the pot. She might then say, 'Go back over there,' and he would. He'd head for the newspaper and he'd sit down. If she said to him, 'Get out, Arnold, until I finish the dinner,' he'd go straight out.

Arnold would never eat rashers, sausages or pudding. He'd never touch pork. My dad would always say, 'You'd think he knew it could be him.' My nanny would put everything together in the bowl, like porridge and water and whatever else was left over from breakfast or dinner, but he would paw the rashers and sausages out of the way. My dad said, 'It was fascinating to watch him eating it and using his foot to shove the pork bits away.'

They'd put potato skins in his dinner, too, but he wouldn't eat them until they'd go soft. They would just sit there in the bowl and my nanny would say to my granddad, 'You have to get rid of them.' He would say, 'No, he'll eat them eventually but only when they are soft.' A few days later, he'd eat them. It was like having a little baby in the house.

Arnold was a great conversationalist. My dad would describe how he'd be sitting there, getting a rub and talking back to you. He'd be grunting away, as if he was having a conversation. He also used to tap on the back door in the morning if he wanted his breakfast. If someone was late up, he'd use his bum to tap twice on the door. You'd know he was hungry and in need of food.

When he was unwell, it was like he was human. Just like a child, he would lie there. They would talk to him and say, 'You are not well,' and he'd soak up the sympathy. My nanny would give him medicine to bring down his temperature. She would put the medicine in his food and he'd eat it, no problem. If you put a tablet in some other animal's food, they wouldn't touch it. But he used to eat it, knowing it would make him well.

He loved his time in the back yard. If it was sunny outside, he'd lie on his back and put all four legs up in the air. He liked the heat coming down on him. The family also used to have a dog, a Cocker Spaniel, as well as Arnold. The two of them got on really well. They played with each other around the yard, chasing each other, and they would sit beside each other when they were resting. But when they would call Arnold, he would come running. He'd run so fast that he'd be slipping around the place.

He'd wait for everyone to come home from school. They used to walk home because they didn't have cars back then. It would take them nearly an hour and they would arrive shortly after four. He'd be waiting outside at the gate. If they were a few minutes late, he'd be out of sorts, wondering where they were. It was like he knew the time of day. My dad always said, 'It was as if Arnold had a watch.' He was really tuned in.

He was also great at guarding the house. If someone came into the yard at nighttime, Arnold would go ballistic. He'd go over to the back door and bang himself off it to let the family inside know that someone was coming in. He'd thump his back off the door and grunt and squeal. He'd recognise neighbours; if they came in he'd go over to them and look for a pet. But if it was someone unusual, he'd go mad.

He was always very clean. There was a place at the end of the yard where they would put horse manure and stuff like that. They would leave it there until a man would come and take it away and spread it. Arnold only went to the toilet there. He'd always walk down there and would never go anywhere else. If he was in the house at nighttime, he'd wake someone up and head off down the yard.

Unfortunately, they also had rats near the house. One day, my dad tried to put his wellies on but Arnold started squealing very loudly. My dad wondered, 'What's wrong with the pig?' Both Arnold and the dog started running over to my father. The dog was pawing at the rubber boot and Arnold was biting the side of it. As my father tried to pick up the boot to put it on, Arnold knocked it over. A rat ran out of it. Both the dog and pig knew the rat was in there and saved my dad.

One night, the family went to bed and Arnold was sleeping outside. He was complaining out the back and my nanny went out to check that everything was OK. She looked around the place and saw nothing. She wondered was he unwell. She said, 'Just go to sleep, Arnold.' She walked back inside and went back to bed. When they got up the next morning, he was gone. He was four years old.

The whole family searched high and low. They split up and looked for him everywhere. They went in all directions. They even went to the mart to see if someone was trying to sell him. But they never found Arnold. All they could think of was that someone had stolen him, probably to make some money.

My dad was so heartbroken. My nanny was, too, especially because she had checked on him during the night and decided to leave him outside. She had even asked my granddad, 'Will I let him in?' But he had said, 'Leave him outside. It's grand weather. There's no need to let him into the house.' My dad always said it was one of my nanny's biggest regrets.

My dad never forgot Arnold. When we were kids, he bought us all piggy banks, which we still have. They are in the sitting-room, on the mantelpiece. I still have old Irish pounds in mine, which I got as pocket money. We have loads of other pig ornaments in the house, like a pig that holds toothpicks and little pig statues. I think our sitting-room is made up of elephants and pigs. I'd say there must be 60 or 70 of them there.

Even today, the pig is my favourite animal. I've been to a pig farm to see them. I wanted to buy a pig, but I don't have the space. My dad always claimed that they are the most intelligent animals you will ever see. He would say, 'Sure, Arnold was only short of using a knife and fork for his dinner.' Or he'd say, 'He was only a few words short of a conversation.' It sounds like Arnold was not only lovable but a bit of a genius.

**DAVE AND MARIAN CURTIN explain how their dog Rover recovered from a bad start to become a genuine superstar.**

We got a Border Collie from an ad in the newspaper in 2005. We thought it was going to be a pup. Dave and our daughter went to pick him up. They brought a small box to hold him in. It was around nine o'clock on a dark, cold evening when they arrived. They saw a sheepdog tearing around the place with an elderly lady after him trying to catch him. Apparently, the dog was after swiping her husband's underpants and when they got the underpants it had been turned into a rag!

When Dave and our daughter asked regarding the pup, the woman said, 'That's him!' My husband decided to take him even though he was about a year old. My daughter said, 'The box is too small. You'll have to ring Mammy.' At this stage, they were about 40 miles away and my husband decided to take him anyway. So off they went home.

We decided to lock Rover in the shed for the night. When we came out in the morning, he was sitting at the back door. He had eaten a hole in the timber shed and escaped but had gone nowhere. That was only the start of it. He turned out to be wild, unruly and terrified of people. He wouldn't go into a car. He would also wet himself.

He was, however, a beautiful black-and-white dog and not vicious. He was a real softie, lovely looking. We found out later that he was a purebred. Gradually, we started training him. It took us about four weeks to train him on a lead and to get him to be not afraid of traffic. Dave then went to a trainer and we started teaching Rover various commands. We said to ourselves, 'We'll train him and see how far we can go.'

We trained him to obey commands in English, Irish and in French. We started with English. We then wondered if he could do it in Irish. After a week or two, he could do everything better in Irish than English. It might have been that Dave's tone is slightly louder in Irish than in English, but there is no doubt he responded better. We also started adding French to his repertoire and he was learning that, as well.

He'd jump the hoop. He was football-crazy and you'd never get a goal past him. We used to dress him in a hat and glasses and he'd perform on stage. He did shows for the old folks and shows at schools. At schools, he'd do the show and we would talk about how to look after pets. He went to playgroups. All the kids loved him. He even did a few stints in pubs.

He could also play the keyboards. He would hit it with the two paws. We went down to Kilkenny one day to buy one. He was so strong with the paws that we knew we would have to replace it within four months. This fellow was showing them to us. We didn't tell him the truth; we said we wanted it for a child of about eight years. He showed us one and we said it was a bit light. 'God, he must be very strong on the keyboards!' the guy said. We eventually found one, and Rover was great at it.

He was a brilliant goalkeeper. He could block the low ones, the high ones, the centre ones. You might score one in 15, but that's about it. He was fantastic. He did a St. Patrick's Day parade once. We dressed him up, he did the loop and we put him into goals. The man who did the commentary said, 'And now, this is Rover, a brilliant goalkeeper, and everybody will see how good he is!' Just before the ball was kicked, didn't a Labrador come from the crowd and walk up to Rover. It was a female. A woman came in and said, 'Sorry! Sorry!' and she took away the Labrador.

Rover went to jelly. It was as if the two of them fell in love. Dave kicked him the ball and he couldn't move. The ball went into the back of the net and everybody laughed. Rover just stood there. Dave kicked it again and he stood there again. He did it a third time and it was the same result. Here was the goalkeeper who was going to block everything but he was like jelly! His heart wasn't in the football anymore that day. We all had a great laugh at what happened.

We also entered him in competitions and he was a massive success. He won the first competition we entered him for. We then started to take him here, there and everywhere. We took him to about 180 shows and he won over 100 first prizes. He won one competition four years in a row. He also qualified for four All-Ireland Spillers championships, which are held at the agricultural show. It's very hard to win and he got down to the final six one year. It was a great achievement.

By the age of four, he was exceptional. He was transformed from a wild dog to an exceptional one. He loved the excitement and he loved travelling off in the car. He loved performing; he'd perform at the drop of a hat. The more you asked him to do, the better he liked it. It was as if he was saying, 'Give me more! Give me more!' He was the genuine article. It was in him. He wanted to please.

We also loved Rover at home. He slept in the kitchen every night. We had a little Dachshund at the time and they would sleep together, with the Dachshund curled up to his bum. She was the boss, but he liked her and they got on brilliantly. He had a great personality and was never aggressive. He was dearly loved by our granddaughter; she adored him and they got on really well.

Unfortunately, it all ended in 2012, when he was seven. He passed away on 12 March that year. He died of bladder cancer. There was blood in his urine. We noticed it on a Friday and on the Monday we were told he would have to be put to sleep. There were tears everywhere. We had really enjoyed our time with him. There was an awful void here for a long time.

People ask us today, 'How is Rover?' When we tell them he has passed away, they are heartbroken. Every time we go to shows, people would be saying, 'Why didn't you bring Rover today?' They would be so sad when they'd hear he had died. He is a big loss to us, too. He had become such a part of us, an extension of us. He was so exceptional, a really wonderful dog. We miss him awfully.

**Antoinette has a rescue horse named Free Spirit, who is as sharp as a tack.**

I only got into horses when I was in my 40s. I always wanted to get into them as a child but my mother would never let me. I thought, 'God! I'd love to get a horse.' I was talking about it for years and saying, 'If only I could think of a hobby, especially one where I didn't need someone to do it with!' It was hard for me to take up a hobby involving other people because of my work. So I investigated it and, once I started taking classes, I loved it. I was 41 at the time.

Eventually, I got some horses of my own. By about four or five years after I started, I had three. I then decided to rescue one. It worried me a lot that so many horses were just being abandoned and left in fields. Horses are not like cats or dogs. You could leave a cat and it will find its owners. They are also sole traders and hunters. Dogs might even find their own way. But horses are different. If one is left in a field, what can he do to survive? He'll never get away. He'll just die.

So that's how this fellow appeared – we rescued him. He was a fine-looking fellow, a good-looking horse. We didn't know what age he was or where he came from. We knew nothing about him. He was a good, strong horse and wasn't starved. He had strong legs on him. We didn't know if anybody had ridden him or anything. But there was something 'free' and 'spirited' about him, so I called him Free Spirit and we decided to keep him as a pet.

From the moment we got him, there was something about his personality that was really outstanding. He was streetwise. He'd always go to the part of the field where the richest grass was. If it was raining in the field, he'd be under the trees while the other fools would be looking at him. If it was sunny, he'd go in from the sun. He knew every trick of the trade. It was unbelievable.

He was definitely unlike the others, who were very precious. They'd be about three-quarters thoroughbred. The funny thing about them was that they didn't like him when they first saw him. It was like they knew he wasn't of 'royal blood'. But he was always up to mischief, very playful and very intelligent. He also had a photographic memory and learned quickly.

I'll give you one example of a habit he learned very fast. When I would see him, I'd tend to clap my hands together. He started doing that – standing up on his back feet and clapping the other ones. We had to stop doing it because he might fall backwards. He was a great mimic in other ways, too. If you started to go up steps, he'd go after you. Most horses won't do that. He was superintelligent.

On one occasion, he was out on the road and was going on a ride. Someone else took him out. He was often a bit bold, but he wouldn't be throwing you off or rearing up. This car came up behind him and started blowing the horn. Most horses would be skittish or go all over the road. But what did he do? He stopped and kicked the headlight of the car with his back legs. It was as if he was saying, 'You do that to me again and that's what you'll get!' He was tough. I nearly died when I heard what had happened.

Another thing started happening when he'd be out grazing in the field. This is the one that really took the biscuit. There are about 12 acres there but it is divided into five separate sections. It is lined by electric fences and surrounded by farmland. The worry always was that he might break into another field and cause a lot of damage. And that's what started happening.

We knew that he was getting out. People had spotted him in nearby fields, running around and squashing pumpkins. They thought there might have been a hole in the ditch or a break in the fence, but there wasn't. We checked the ditch and we also checked the electric fence and we found nothing. We couldn't figure it out.

Then, one evening, he was spotted. There he was rolling himself under the electric fence while coming back in from the neighbouring field. He was down on his hunkers, lying sideways and rolling himself under. He was keeping his legs down because he knew what would happen if he touched the fence. It was unbelievable.

What he had been doing was watching us when we would be down in the field. Instead of unhooking the electric cable, which we now do, we were ducking underneath it. This is the way he learned how to do it. He would just get down, like us, and roll underneath the fence. The other fools would be standing there looking at him. After that, all the fences had to be lowered. He hasn't done it since, touch wood.

I think he is very bright. Not only did he learn how to escape underneath the fence but he would never do it when you were watching – he'd be too cute for that. He is definitely something else. I often think he knows he has been rescued. I also think that he's the sort of horse that if you had him in a garden near the house he'd be coming into the house and following you around.

All my horses are different. In fact, I think no two horses are the same. One might be good at dressage, another one good at showjumping, yet another for cross-country, maybe another for hacking out. But he's multi-skilled. As someone said, 'He's the best of all of them.' They are all special in their own way, but he can do everything. He is an amazing horse, with a highly-appropriate name, Free Spirit.

**MICHAEL FERGUSON recalls two dogs, Rex and Shep, who were wonderful footballers. They brightened up his life almost four decades ago.**

Rex didn't belong to me, but that didn't prevent the dog from believing that I belonged to him. He was the larger of two collies who lived near me in a place called Mount St. James, Greenore, County Louth. It was out in the country. Across the road from our house was a sort of farmyard and Rex belonged to the farmer. The problem was that he wasn't any good with sheep; he was just a pet dog hanging around.

He became so fond of me that he thought I owned him or that he owned me. He adopted me even though I was working in Dublin and would only be home at the weekend. He was a lovely dog, dark with brown stripes, and white under the chin. He had a lovely temperament.

There was another collie, called Shep, who lived about 100 yards down the hill. He was a smaller dog, black and white, and also had a lovely temperament. His owners didn't use him for anything, either. He was such an intelligent dog that every time he heard my car coming home on a Friday evening he would perk up, run like hell and come straight up to the house.

That's when our football matches would begin. Shep would make a beeline for our garden, where there was an outhouse that usually contained a football. He would push the door open, bring the ball out with his two paws and roll it out into the garden. He would have it there before I switched off the ignition in the car. He would then stand back four or five paces and he would invite me to kick the ball.

I would lob the ball and he would jump in the air and head it back. He would be trying to snap it with his teeth, but it would be too big for him so it would look like he was heading it. Other times, he would push the ball in front of him through the garden. He'd end up bringing it back to me, then he'd back off a few paces and we'd be off again.

Rex would hear the barking and excitement, so he'd come running from the house across the road. Straightaway, great tackling would ensue between the two of them for possession of the ball. Rex was the larger of the two collies and he lacked the finesse and agility of his smaller companion, so he would compensate for his lack of skill by his sheer doggedness – excuse the pun – as a tackler. This he would do by holding on to the ball with his two front paws and deny any attempt to dislodge it.

This tactic didn't go down well with Shep, whose crafty ploy was to attack Rex's tail. This would result in Rex turning on his attacker and leaving the ball free for further action either through me or Shep. Even though they were fierce protagonists, there was never any viciousness displayed between them, only a mutual frustration at the very different football styles they exhibited.

This could have gone on all day, but I would have to break off to go in for my evening meal. When I did so, they would sit patiently side by side awaiting my return. When I came back out, off we would go again. Their energy was inexhaustible and they would play forever if given the opportunity.

Rex also loved going with me when I went fishing, although his tendency to bark incessantly and occasionally swim around the other fishermen didn't endear him to them at all. He would usually accompany me by running beside my bike and then splash about merrily and noisily in the sea while I prepared my shiniest German Sprat to catch some of the plentiful mackerel in Carlingford Lough.

The only problem was that Rex delighted in taunting and challenging two dogs much larger and more formidable than he was and who were confined behind the high walls of a house on the shoreline. The nub of this particular story centres on the height of the wall, which on the roadside amounted to approximately four feet but on the garden side it sank to a depth of six feet. As long as Rex remained on the road, he could look across the wall at his enemies while they could only see him by jumping in a bouncing motion. In other words, he was safe.

One evening, however, the usual confrontation came to a big crisis point when Rex's bravado overcame his better judgement and, to my utter horror and dismay, he took a running jump, cleared the wall and entered the very jaws of death. The two Alsatians, whose dinner had just landed in their territory, got ready to tear their uninvited guest limb from limb. I thought they were going to kill him.

Suddenly, like a soaring eagle, though really a soaring collie, Rex took a run at the wall and cleared it by at least two feet – that's eight feet in all – thus creating an Olympic record which will never be repeated in dog high-jump lore! You could see the other dogs jumping up but unable to get over the wall. To insult them, Rex, on realising that he was free from any followers, returned to the wall, gave three barks and then headed for the shore. I would dearly love to have Doctor Dolittle translate that victory speech!

We eventually left Greenore for good and I didn't get back very much. It killed me to think that I was going away and I wouldn't see them again. In many ways, they were part of my growing up. But what can you do? Life goes on – unfortunately, very, very fast – and we all change our homes and even change our friends.

But the memories of those two dogs live on, frozen moments in time, and I loved the two of them. I frequently wonder what happened to them and I wonder if they would have remembered me if I had ever seen them again. I hope they would.

I sometimes go back to Greenore and I pass my old house. One of the gardens where we played is now covered in concrete. Things have moved on. But they were great, halcyon days, and I know that if dogs have a heaven then both Rex and Shep have a wonderful home. I'll certainly be watching out for them when I arrive up there, playing football or, in Rex's case, annoying Alsatians!

**MARGARET WILSON gives us an insight to her family's smaller pets, including a kamikaze hamster called Bubbles.**

We always had pets when my children were growing up. We had them from when the children were three or four, right on up. We had a selection of hamsters and several goldfish. We had a guinea pig called Patch. We even had mice. There were always pets of some description in the house.

We got the mice from a teacher who had white mice in her classroom. When the summer break came, she said she didn't trust the students to take them home because of what their parents' reactions might be. She asked her own mother, but she said, 'No mice are coming into this house.' So she asked me would I take them. I said, 'I'll take them.'

I did ask, however, if they were male and female and I was told, 'They are both the same!' I took them home and placed them on top of the piano. One Sunday morning, I was hoovering and I heard some squeaks. When I looked into the cage, eight little babies were there. They didn't have hair on them or they didn't have fur; they were just like pieces of pink soap. I got homes for every one of them.

We also ended up having three hamsters, but not all at the same time. We had Hamlet, who was very handsome and almost black. We had Pinky Paws, who was conventional and didn't do too much out of the ordinary. And then we had Bubbles, the acrobat, who was the exceptional one.

Hamsters are adorable little creatures, but their lives are very short. They don't live much longer than about three years and then they die. They come and go. You get attached to them and then they disappear from your life.

They also can do strange things. I think it was Pinky Paws who went missing one time. We noticed she was gone. I thought she had got out. Then, one morning, we were at breakfast and we heard a rustling sound. We found Pinky Paws in the Corn Flakes box! She had moved in. I'm afraid the Corn Flakes had to be thrown out.

I had a very soft-hearted son around the time we had Hamlet. The hamster died, one day, while my son was at school. I had to make up a wonderful story that I had given Hamlet to an explorer and he was going to release him into the wild. I came up with all sorts of rubbish. He accepted it because he was so young. Otherwise, he would have been in tears.

I'm not sure where my children got Bubbles, probably from one of the pet shops. I always refer to her as a 'she' but I have no idea what sex the hamster really was. We used to keep her in a cage in the living-room. She would be in the cage during the day, going round and round on the wheel. She seemed very happy doing that.

We used to let her out for a while in the evening. We did this with the other hamsters, too. They would come and sit on your shoulder. The only problem was that when we would let Bubbles out, she used to climb up the curtains, right to the very top, sit on the rail for a minute and then fling herself off.

She would fly down to the floor, onto the carpet, and knock herself out completely. Whenever she was out of the cage, she would do this. The first time she did it, I thought she was dead. I gave her heart massage and she came around. What did she do then? She climbed up the curtains and flung herself off again! She used to do it all the time.

We called her 'The Kamikaze Hamster'. We named her after the Japanese airmen who flew their planes into ships. I have absolutely no idea why she was really doing it. I mean, she would knock herself out completely. Maybe in a former life she had been a bird!

Bubbles got old and she eventually died. After that, we never owned hamsters again. Now that my children are adults and in their own homes, they don't have hamsters, either. Instead, they both have dogs. My granddaughter has a Labradoodle, which is a big dog, and my son has a chocolate Labrador, which is also quite big. Nobody has returned to keeping hamsters. I wonder if the memory of Bubbles flying through the air has anything to do with that!

**MAUREEN McCARTHY outlines how her pet dog Cuddles made up to her after she did something wrong.**

Cuddles was a Skye Terrier. My friend gave me her as a present as a little puppy. She was gorgeous, with lovely markings, big brown eyes, and she was a shade of reddish-brown. She was also very long, with short legs. My brother used to say that she was so long she must have had an extra pair of legs in the middle. She would break your heart.

Her sister was very placid and easygoing, just like her owner. But Cuddles took my personality and was very hyper and had to be involved in everything. She disliked children because they took attention away from her. Occasionally, my friend would come over for a glass of wine in the kitchen. Cuddles would get the idea that no one was talking to her, so she would climb up on the table and spread her long body across it. Then we'd have to talk about her.

One time, back in 1990, I remember I was trying to give up cigarettes. Cuddles was about four years old. I was either in the kitchen or in the living-room. The next thing, I heard this awful commotion at the front door. The postman had been trying to put letters into the letterbox, but Cuddles was waiting for him. This was before we had a porch. The letterbox was at the side of the door and Cuddles was obviously waiting there.

I opened the front door and the poor postman was standing outside. He was a temporary postman. Cuddles had bitten his fingers and he was bleeding badly. There was a lot of blood. She could be very vicious like that. I brought him in and said, 'I'm so sorry.' He said, 'I'll have to report this.' He could see that I was very upset. So he said, 'Don't worry. I'll just go to the doctor.'

I said to him, 'Are you watching the World Cup later tonight down in the pub?' He said, 'I am.' So I gave him some money to have a few drinks on me. He was very nice. Somebody else could have made it very difficult. He could have brought it further and got her put down, but he was a very decent man.

After he left, I gave out hell to the dog. I had already put her into the bedroom. She ran into the closet and hid on me. I said to her, 'You're a very, very bold girl.' She put her head and tail down. She was clearly very upset, and rightly so. I then went off to get some cigarettes to calm my nerves.

When I came back, I opened the door and there was Cuddles sitting in the middle of the hall. She had all these cuddly little toys in a pile and was sitting on top of them. There must have been eight, nine or ten toys in the pile. They were the sort of cuddly toys that the kids had in their beds and that were around the house. She had brought them all down and was trying to make up to me. She was sitting there with the hangdog eyes.

I knew immediately that she was trying to say she was sorry. It was as if she was saying, 'Will you forgive me just this time?' Once you saw that face, what else could you do? I just had to forgive her. So I said, 'You're a good girl!' and petted her and was all over her. We made up and, needless to say, she got away with it again. It wasn't long before she returned to her normal self and she was back in the bed that night.

Even at the time, I knew exactly what she was at. She would have known what she was doing and that she could get around me. She knew me better than I knew myself. But I also knew that she would do the very same thing again. And that's what happened. I had been telling my five-year-old son about the postman. One day, as he was coming home from school, he decided to play a little game and put his finger in through the letterbox. Unfortunately, Cuddles was waiting there for him. She never learned her lesson.

She died on 4 October 2002, on the feast day of St. Francis. She was 15 years old and was taking strokes and losing power. I couldn't be cruel to her, so I had to put her down. But the date she died was strange. I'm not an overly-religious person, but I'm a great one for lighting candles and I always thought it was meant to be. I felt it was amazing.

I still think of her a lot. She was a beautiful dog, really full of character and we all loved her. I have a shrine to her, with photographs and a poster up of a dog like her. I also have a photo of her in a Santa Claus hat. I'm reminded in other ways, too. Some years later, the postman came back and he said, 'Mrs. McCarthy, do you remember me?' I said, 'No, I don't.' He said, 'Don't you remember? Your dog bit me.' I then recognised him immediately and said, 'It's OK! The dog is dead, you're safe!'

**PATRICIA ROCHE describes the charms of looking after a chatterbox pet parrot.**

We were at a party and there was a guy there who was talking to my husband. He said, 'I have two African grey parrots and I'm trying to re-home them.' My husband, without consulting me, said, 'Oh, I'll have them!' A week later, we got a phone call telling us, 'The two birds are in a taxi.' They were on their way.

These two birds turned up, Rocky and Jack. They were grey with red tails. Rocky was the woman, Jack was the man. Jack had a wonderful personality, but from the beginning he was a victim. Rocky really bullied him. She didn't like him and he didn't like her. He was frightened of her.

Jack got so badly depressed that he had to be put on medication. He started to bite his leg and it got badly infected. There were all sorts of problems. We had to separate them and get two cages. Unfortunately, one day, I had the back door open and Jack flew away. We couldn't find him even though we searched everywhere.

Rocky is very different to what Jack used to be. Jack had been great at all the sounds. He would do the doorbell, the telephone and the washing machine. Rocky is more the chatterbox. She is the gossipy type and can imitate anyone.

She must have been somewhere, at one stage, where there was a building site. She refers to someone called Nigel. She shouts, 'Nigel! Come over here, you lazy git!' She keeps roaring, 'Nigel!' She goes into that rant now and again.

She laughs if you're in trouble. Maybe you've spilled something and she will go, 'Ha! Ha! Ha! Ha! Ha! Ha! Ha! Ha!' It's a screechy laugh, really loud. She also imitates the phone and she will laugh when you pick it up, knowing she has made a fool of you. But she is nice, as well, and smart. We have her now for over 12 years and we're very fond of her.

She can cause a lot of trouble. One day, my husband was on the phone trying to get clearance to do an important job. He was in the hall, talking to someone important. Rocky started making some rude noises in the background. She would have known what she was doing. My husband never got the job!

There was another incident that I will never forget. I had opened the cage to let her stand on top of it or fly about. She isn't very good at flying; she hasn't got confidence. I was out in the kitchen and heard an ambulance. I thought, 'That seems louder than it normally should be.' I was wondering what was going on. I went into the front room, where Rocky was, to find out.

Rocky had flown about, got trapped behind the television and couldn't take off. She was in with all the wires and the space was too cramped. She did the ambulance sound to catch my attention. She must have known that the ambulance meant distress and she had the intelligence to seek help. That was so funny.

She also comes up with the strangest of things. Recently, my sister was in our house and we were talking about money or the economy. Suddenly, Rocky comes out with, 'All I've got is a fiver!' She makes a lot of connections. She is really bright.

On another occasion, my stepson was watching the television. She asked him, 'What are you watching?' He said, 'I'm watching the football.' She said, 'What's the score?' He suddenly said, 'Oh, my God! I'm talking to a bird!' But she does like TV, and when David Attenborough's programmes are on she watches them intensely.

She's really very entertaining. One morning, it was dark and I came down and took the cover off the cage and she growled at me like a dog. It was like, 'Don't disturb me, I'm asleep!' So she is amusing and she's always prattling away about something.

The chances are she will outlive us. They can live up to 80 or 90 years or more. Because of that, we had to write her into our will. We have willed her to my sister. But that's OK. My sister loves to chat and the two of them get on very well. If we go first, they will have a bright future together!

**Priscilla Donovan, who comes originally from America, reveals how her dog Buddy had an operatic voice to match Caruso.**

I got Buddy a couple of months after I moved to Ireland. I got him from a neighbour whose dog had pups. His mother was a Golden Retriever, but the litter came out black. We don't know about the father; he was passing through town, I guess.

He was a big, beautiful dog, extremely friendly, with long black hair and a wonderful temperament. My husband Tom and I both adored him. Once he knew you and knew you were OK, he wouldn't stop rubbing and petting you and even putting his head in your lap. Everyone who came to the house loved him doing that – putting his head in their lap.

He loved to play more than he loved to eat. He was very smart and he'd make up games. He would chase birds that were swimming in the sea. Of course, they would just keep swimming farther and farther away and he'd keep going after them to no avail. He'd also bark at gulls on the cliff to get them down and then chase them. He loved having fun.

He was also very protective of me and the house. If someone came to the door, he would bark until I told him it was OK. If we were walking in the woods and a stranger was approaching, he would go ahead and bark until I gave him the signal. I would tell him, 'It's OK! It's OK!' and he would stop.

I am a trained singer and I have done a lot of singing in my life. I've been in operas and musicals, especially in America. I was in a Benjamin Britten opera called *Albert Herring*, playing a Queen Victoria type of lady. I was in Mozart's *Così fan tutte*, playing Despina. I was in the musicals *A Little Night Music* and *The Threepenny Opera*. Singing is very much in my blood.

Because of my musical background, I would often be singing around the house. If I heard something on the radio, it might set me off. If I got up and it was a beautiful morning, I might sing Oh, What a Beautiful Mornin' from *Oklahoma!* I also might be rehearsing as I did quite a few shows in Ireland.

Buddy would join in with my singing. He had a great, strong voice, with a large range, high and low. First, you would just hear a tiny little whine, with the mouth pursed. Then his voice would get louder. When I would go into the high register, he would throw his head way back and howl along. We might start laughing and that would bring it to an end. Alternatively, I might keep singing and he would sing as long as I did.

He was a baritone, but he could go into falsetto at the top and then go up real high. He really liked the high register. That might have been because he mainly recognised the higher notes. For example, when I'd be out swimming with him, and if I wanted him to hear me, I'd call his name and would use my higher voice and he'd hear me. The explanation might have been as simple as that.

When I was teaching singing, here at the house, he might join in. There was one girl who had looked after him briefly when he was a puppy. He remembered her after all those years. When she was having her lessons, he would sit next to her so that her hand would be resting on his head.

When I'd take her up the scales, into the stratosphere, Buddy would start off. When she would go high, he would go high. If she came back down, he'd come back down. Once it got to the low register, he would stop. We would be roaring with laughter. The singing would have to stop for a while.

Other people saw him do this, as well. I used to take him out to a place near a ferry and a lot of tourists would be around.

They would watch him go into the water, chasing sticks. I might give him commands in German – I had studied it, as I sang in German – and he would obey them. Oh, how they would laugh! I think he sang for them a couple of times and they were amazed. There are photographs of him all over Europe!

As he got older, he went into decline. He had trouble standing up and walking. His hearing started to go and he didn't sing in ages. We had a young vet come out and she did chiropractic treatments on him. It helped him enormously. One of the first things he did after the first treatment was sing. I sang to him and he threw back his head and sang back to me. I think the treatment gave him another year.

He then started getting cancer. He had tumours. I knew we weren't going to treat him because he was too old. I had always promised him that I would be with him to the end. I always said to him, 'I'm never going to leave you.' But I knew he was ready to go when he started turning away from his food and the singing had stopped.

The night before he died, as weak as he clearly was, he forced himself to get up and come over to me. I was saying, 'You don't have to do that. Stay! Stay! I'll come to you.' But he came to me, to be with me and to be rubbed. Then he went back to his bed and didn't get up anymore. He was 15 and a half at the time.

He had a very quiet, peaceful death. I stayed with him to the end. I rubbed his head and I actually sang to him. I always sang a song to him, 'My Buddy lies over the ocean. My Buddy lies over the sea.' So I sang that. He didn't move, but his tail wagged. And that was the end of Buddy.

# DOG DAZE

If you aspire to being a world leader then you had better acquire a dog. Alexander the Great owned Peritas, believed to have been a Bulldog; Adolf Hitler was close to Blondi, his German Shepherd; John F. Kennedy had Charlie, his Welsh Terrier; Bill Clinton kept Buddy, a Labrador Retriever.

American President Harry Truman emphasised a dog's friendship and loyalty when he commented, 'If you want a friend in Washington, get a dog.' French President Charles de Gaulle concurred: 'The better I get to know men, the more I find myself loving dogs.'

Another American President, Woodrow Wilson, noted wisely, 'If a dog will not come to you after having looked you in the face, you should go home and examine your conscience.' Dogs are, indeed, man's best friends, loyal, affectionate and providers of bundles of love, as we will see in the following stories.

**OLIVE owned a dog named Podge, who was less than amused when excluded from a family holiday.**

We got Podge a good many years ago. Initially, we got him for my elderly aunt who lived on her own down in Carlow. He was just a little puppy, black and white, with a kind face, and he was so affectionate. He was half-Labrador and half-sheepdog. Everyone who met him loved him. I loved him, too, and would meet him on my visits up and down to Carlow. I worked in Dublin at the time.

My aunt owned another dog, called Jake. Jake was the older dog, more dominant and was part-Alsatian. Podge would play with Jake, swing off his tail and bite his ears. That was grand as long as Jake would put up with it. Every so often, however, Jake would have enough and there would be a fight.

One night, there was a fight so bad that I had to close the kitchen door and shut them out in the garden. I had to go out with the hose, but nothing would stop them. Eventually, Jake, the victor, arrived in. I told everyone to keep back and not to go near him. You could see he had been in a frenzy. He walked in and sat down at his place in front of the fire.

I went out, brokenhearted, to pick up the body of Podge. I really feared the worst. But Podge suddenly lifted his head and trotted up the yard to me. He was in bits. I got the vet, who sewed him up and put him together again. I then had to ask the vet to get another home for Jake because the fighting had got so bad. It was so sad.

I would meet Podge every time I went down to Carlow. I noticed, on Sunday mornings, he would wake up and make a lot of noise to get out. It was always around eight o'clock. Much later, a man told me that he used to see Podge not just on Sunday mornings but on other mornings, too, trotting up the road and heading off to a girlfriend about quarter of a mile away. It was obviously a regular date. How he survived such a narrow and dangerous road was an absolute miracle.

My aunt eventually died, so we brought Podge back with us to Dublin. He was about five at that stage. Everyone in the family became attached to him. On one occasion, one of my sons was upset over something and he lifted Podge up into his bunk bed. When I went into the room, I found Podge with his paws wrapped around my son. He was a lovely dog.

I became very attached to Podge and he became attached to me. He wanted to go everywhere I went. He would jump in the car, get in the back and wedge himself under the front seat. One day, I was late and rushing to work and I just couldn't get him out of the car. I had to bring him with me. All that day, I brought him out food, took him for a wee, got him a dish of water and, of course, also left the car window open. He never jumped in the car again. He was a quick learner.

There was one occasion when I decided to take the family away for the weekend. The only problem was that I had no one to look after Podge. I was forced to ask my ex-husband if he would take him. He said, 'Yes, I will.' It was very good of him. I knew that there would be no stress involved because my ex-husband knew him. So off we went, although I was worried that Podge would pine a bit and miss me.

We eventually came home after a wonderful weekend and I couldn't wait to get Podge back. Finally, my ex-husband arrived at the door with the dog. The door opened. I was standing at the end of the hall with my arms outstretched and full of joy. I said, 'Podge!' But he tossed his head and walked briskly past me, with his head held high, out through the breakfast-room and into the garden.

Podge was clearly devastated that I had left him and he was letting me know. I couldn't believe it. I was quite taken aback, much to the amusement of my ex-husband. I think he has dined out for years on that story. Eventually, Podge came around and he was fine. I have a memory of the event – a photo which my ex-husband gave me of Podge sitting in his back garden while on holidays during our weekend away.

Eventually, Podge got old and he wasn't able to walk up the stairs at night. He always slept at the end of the bed. He would have died trying to climb the stairs rather than stay downstairs. He just had to go up. One of my sons had to bend his knees and very gently lift him with both arms from underneath. My son would stagger up the stairs and put him gently on the landing. Podge would then trot into my bedroom.

One night, my daughter was having a twenty-first birthday party. When I came home from work, things were in full swing. I thought I would go up to bed and keep out of their way. My sons couldn't be found to carry Podge up. One of my daughter's friends said, 'Don't worry. I'll carry him up for you.' Before I could do or say anything, he put his two arms the wrong way around the dog's middle and Podge, who was always incredibly gentle, bit him on the ear.

My daughter came into the hall and saw her friend with the blood running down from his ear. And there was I saying, 'That's not the way you lift him!' That was all I was concerned with – the dog, not the friend's ear. The poor fellow had been doing his best, but all I was concerned about was Podge. My daughter was absolutely mortified.

He eventually died. He was hardly able to walk at the end. He was at least 16, maybe a little more, and he was weary. I was so distraught after he passed away. He had really been part of the family and such good company. Dogs don't care when you put on weight or get old – their love is unconditional. And Podge's love certainly was like that.

I know it's strange but I remember every so often, at night, he would come to the narrow space at the side of the bed and I would put my hand on his head and tell him he was such a good dog. He was happy after I did that and he would reverse out and lie down on the rug at the end of the bed. I know this sounds crackers, but when I'd put my hand on his head I would feel a surge of energy in my hand as I told him what a good boy he was. It sounds strange, but it's true. He was very special, an amazing dog, and I will never forget him.

**MARY RYAN recalls a lovely collie who possessed all the instincts of her breed along with a wonderful personality.**

Amber was a black collie cross with a little white breast. I got her when she was five to six months old and I called her Amber because what else could you call a black dog with amber eyes if you lived in Kilkenny? She became my black-and-amber dog in the Kilkenny colours. I thought I was being really clever until I met so many other Ambers throughout the county – golden Labradors, black-and-tan tiny terriers and so on.

She had immense character and her own ways. She had that collie thing. They are very sensible dogs and very serious about the job they do. They guard you and they herd. For example, when I'd bring her to the Phoenix Park in Dublin she would put all the ducks into the water because they belonged in the water. The birds belonged up in the trees, so she would chase them up there. They flew, so that is where they had to be, up in trees.

When we would be in a house, she could not relax until she had herded everyone into one room. She would only feel she had done her job when everyone would congregate in the kitchen or the living-room. Only then would she sit down and relax. While everyone was in different rooms, she would keep moving around because her job wasn't done. We all had to be penned in. That was her instinct from the collie in her.

We live near a nature reserve where the mallards breed and where there are swans and coots and water hens and rats. She would sit for a whole day watching the rats. She was fascinated by them. She wouldn't chase them; she would just sit there and watch. She also never chased cats. That was probably because we had a cat called Tiger and they were the best of friends. There was nothing she loved better than playing with cats and curling up with them.

She had other interesting habits. One day, I went to Dublin and didn't take her with me. My neighbour minded her for the day. Another dog killed a mouse and took it into her house. Amber sat in her hall beside the dead mouse for the entire day. She did that until I came back and she showed me the dead mouse. She wouldn't eat or drink; she just guarded the little mouse until I returned.

On another occasion, when I was in Dublin, I left her two sausages in her doggie bowl. I travelled to Dublin by the eight o'clock morning bus and returned on the nine o'clock evening bus. I got to my house sometime around 11 o'clock. There she was with the two sausages still in her bowl along with her doggie biscuits. She stood in front of me, her feet planted squarely, and barked and barked, telling me off. She then picked up a sausage, flung it up in the air, went out for a wee and came back in and ate the two sausages!

She also had a thing about the postman. She'd bark at him from inside the house. After he left, she'd grab whatever he had put through the letterbox. You could see she felt she had got rid of him. She'd come to me, wagging her tail, as if to say, 'I've got rid of him again!' She'd then go into the sitting-room and look out the window and stay barking as he went into other houses. I often felt that if she got a bite of a postman, her reason for living would be fulfilled!

The thing I remember most about Amber is that she was so kind. In the morning, she would come to me while I was in bed. I might have my feet sticking out of the bed. She would lick me on the sole of my foot so gently. If I didn't raise myself up, she'd lick me on the hand. If I still didn't respond, she would climb on the bed and place herself alongside me, really gently, with no leaping or jumping, and lick me on the face. Once I moved, she'd slide down the stairs and go *woof*, meaning, 'Let me out!'

One day, when she was nearly 13 years old, she became very unwell. It was early in the morning, about quarter to one. She went under a little coffee table and was making funny noises. I felt something had happened inside her head, in her brain. She wasn't bleeding or anything else, just restless, pacing around, bumping off my legs and also bumping into things. She couldn't sleep.

I said, 'I'll take her out for a walk.' She went outside the door and I ducked back in to get an umbrella and an anorak because it had started to rain. When I came back out, she was gone; she had vanished into thin air. There was no sign of her. I searched for hours and hours. I went everywhere but couldn't find her. I went home and I prayed to God she was OK.

At about quarter to seven in the morning, I went looking for her again. A man told me he had seen a black dog and told me where he had seen it. I got there at about quarter past seven. There was Amber, sitting on the verge of the road, with the cars going around her, looking very unwell. Her eyes were flat, there was no recognition. She didn't know I was there and she didn't know she was saturated.

Another man helped me and lifted her up. He actually took off his fleece jacket and wrapped her in it to keep her warm. He took us home. When we got there, she didn't even know how to lie down. She began to have convulsions. Her personality was completely gone. There was nothing left of Amber.

I brought her to the vet, who advised me to put her down. I thought, 'She has had a good life, with no unkindness, and she has done everything she wanted to do.' I felt that if I was Amber I wouldn't want to be left struggling. I kissed her on her head and said goodbye. She had never liked her paws touched, but I held her paws and rubbed her little footpads with my thumb. Then the vet put her to sleep, and she slept quietly.

I miss her badly. I cope when I have to cope, but then the sorrow comes. I sometimes just want to feel her, feel her lick my hand, and rub her head. I don't want a memory of her; I just want her. There's an absence, a knowing I'm never going to see her and hear her again. It can be so painful.

I still have photos of her in my phone and bits of video, although I'm sorry I don't have more. Because of the photos, I can still see her little face and I have lovely memories of her. But she was irreplaceable. The pain may ease with time, but out of the blue I still get that longing for her and I want her and then I have some tears. She was just my Amber.

MARGARET WILSON **talks about the distant, conniving, selfish, unaffectionate dog she loved to bits.**

Finn came to us as a stray. She followed my daughter home one very wet evening. I felt a bit sorry for her, so I threw a piece of carpet into the garage and gave her the remains of our Sunday dinner. That was a bad idea! We left the garage side door open and expected she would be gone in the morning.

When we woke in the morning, she was still there. For quite a few days after that, every time I came home from work she would be sitting on our doorstep. She was haunting our house. Up to then, I had always shied away from having a dog because my husband and I worked full-time. But this dog was determined to come and live with us and have a home with us, so eventually we capitulated and said, 'Right! We'll keep her!'

It turned out that she was a sort of cross between a German Shepherd and a collie, although I always thought she had a bit of Greyhound in her, as well. We knew nothing about dogs and we thought she was a male. We called her Finn because of that. After a while, my next-door neighbour enlightened me that this was no male – it was a female. We thought about changing the name to Fionnuala but she had got used to Finn so we stuck with it.

Right from the beginning, she wasn't an affectionate dog. She disdained affection. She was the exact opposite of Greyfriars Bobby. She was conniving and selfish, and she ran the house as if it was her own fiefdom. She moved into the kitchen, then she progressed to the landing, and she would have dearly liked to be sleeping on the bed but I drew the line at that.

She insinuated herself into our lives. She did whatever she liked and wasn't obedient. She would sprawl out on the settee. We would say, 'Get up!' and push her, but she was a big dog and wouldn't move. She would take up her position so close to the fire that she would singe. You could smell her fur singeing. Keeping the heat away from us wouldn't bother her in the least.

She really was distant and cool. I had a very bad fall one day while taking clothes in from the garden. I tripped down some steps at the back of the house. I knew I was going to pass out because I was in such pain. I just made it to the back door when I collapsed.

Finn was out in the garden at the time. My last recollection was of her walking over my prone body on her way into the house. When I came to, she was lying in front of a lovely fire in the living-room, not one bit perturbed that I was sprawled half in and half out at the back of the house!

She terrified people coming to visit. She would bare her teeth and growl, and she had the bark of a German Shepherd. She could be quite scary, but she never bit anybody. I think she was too crafty for that. She was far too thought-out; she thought everything out.

She did bite my husband's pants, though. That happened when my son was on a curfew. He was doing exams and his father told him he had to be in at a certain time. He broke the curfew and was quite late one night, and my husband chased him upstairs. He wouldn't have touched him; he just chased him. Finn got the seat of my husband's pants and tore it to shreds. She didn't go into the flesh, just the pants.

She also terrified two purebred Doberman Pinschers living next-door to us. They were absolutely beautiful animals. Finn burrowed her way through the hedge into their garden. She backed them down and then ate their dinner! She was quite a character. She had a tough streak.

On the other hand, she could be easily scared. Further up the street, there was an epileptic Chihuahua. This tiny little dog would bounce up and down on these little fish legs and Finn would be terrified. When I would take her out on the lead, she always positioned me between her and the Chihuahua, even though she was bigger. She really didn't like this little dog!

We also had a break-in once. I came home from work at lunchtime and realised that the glass in the front door had been smashed. I went in and didn't know if the people were still upstairs. Finn was in her bed in the kitchen. I got her out and pushed her towards the stairs. I said, 'Go on up!' But she got in behind me and cried. It turned out that the thieves were long gone, but Finn wasn't going up the stairs or defending me, no way!

We looked after her well. I know better now that dogs should not consume chocolate. But my husband, when he was bringing home sweets to the family, would also bring her a little bag of raspberry ruffles. She would eat them; she loved them. They didn't do her any harm. That was her little treat.

We also used to walk Finn and when she was younger she enjoyed it. When she got older, she changed her view. When she was around 15, I had a minor operation and was told to walk three miles every night. She knew when I put the coat on that she would be heading out. She would hide under the table. She had become lazy.

She had a very serious accident once. My family had a small seaside place and we went there on holiday. My husband and son had gone in the car into the village for ice cream. What I didn't know was that Finn had followed the car up the lane. My husband and son didn't know, either. She ran out onto the road and a car hit her.

Finn limped up the lane and the man followed her. He came to our door and asked if we had a black-and-tan dog. I said yes. He said, 'She ran right in front of me and I think she is over there, under that bush.' When we looked at her, she was in a dreadful way. We wrapped her up in a rug and the man took us into the village, to the vet.

The vet didn't know whether he was going to treat her or not. He said he would keep her overnight, but she was there for three or four nights. He eventually said he did what wasn't so much a stitching job as an embroidery job and, after a few weeks, she bounced back. The vet said that if she had been a purebred, she probably wouldn't have survived; he thought mongrels were tougher.

We had her for 17 years, but then she got cancer. The vet said he could remove the lump, but he reckoned she would only last a few more months. We couldn't put her through that. At that stage, her teeth were ground down, as well. When she was out walking, she always selected the largest rock she could find and she brought it home in her jaws. I don't know how she carried them. The whole thing had affected her teeth and she would have needed some of them out, as well.

My husband and I decided the best thing for her would be to have her put down. We held her and we held each other, and we cried and bawled. The vet put her to sleep and we had her cremated. We collected her ashes. She had been very fond, in the summertime, of sleeping under a particular rose tree. That's where we buried her ashes, along with her lead and her bowl and her toys. They all went under the rose bush.

Even though we don't live there anymore, she is still with us in memory. We have photographs of her and we will always remember her. She was determined to have a home with us and she wasn't going anywhere else. She had stayed with us for 17 years and we had loved her to bits. But like people, I suppose, she had her own personality. Some can be a bit cool, and Finn was definitely cool, there's no doubt about that!

**PAULA CUNNINGHAM reflects on her Jack Russell dogs, especially Bertie who has passed away.**

We owned a Jack Russell for 12 years. We got him as a pup and we called him Bertie. We couldn't think of a name for him, but Bertie Ahern was on the news one night and the little pup ran up to the TV set. That's how he got christened Bertie. I don't know if that's a good thing or a bad thing, but the name suited him.

He was a very handsome dog, with perfect markings. He was ginger and white. He really loved his food as a puppy, so he was a bit chubby and he stayed that way all his life. He had instant likeability. He loved everybody and was a real gentleman. He would wait for you to walk out the door in front of him. He loved music, as well. If you started to sing, he'd start singing, too.

We got him along with his sister Gypsy. They came from the same litter but they had two very different personalities. Gypsy was quiet and kept to herself. She was independent and did her own thing. She was also selfish and was the boss of the two of them. Sometimes, Bertie would try to lie in beside her in the bed next to the fire, but she wouldn't allow him because she might want to sprawl out. He would accept that; he was so accepting of everything.

They were funny when they were young. I remember the first time they discovered snow. They were wandering around in it and tasting it, galloping about, looking as if they were asking, 'What's this stuff?' I also remember when they first discovered rain. I took them for a walk beside the river, one day, and it rained. They were both sheltering and looking up at me as if it was my fault. At least, on that occasion, they shared something in common – blaming me!

Bertie loved every day. He embraced each day with wonder, enthusiasm and total joy. He would jump into situations as if he was declaring, 'This is me!' He wasn't like a normal Jack Russell, which is often perceived as being cross. For example, we had a donkey in the field beside us and she would bend down to sniff Bertie. He wouldn't be annoyed; instead, he'd lick her nose and give her kisses. He was full of love.

He always seemed to be looking for the positives. If he went for a walk on the beach and some unsavoury dogs were there, he'd just wag his tail and walk around them. Yet he was tough enough when he needed to be. There was an older gentleman who owned a Jack Russell which he had rescued from a pound. I volunteered to look after his dog, Scamp, when he was away. One day, when we were walking on the beach, another dog tried to attack Scamp but Bertie dived in to help. He wasn't going to let his team down.

He wanted to get everybody happy. If there was a happy mood in the house, he'd be galloping around in circles just to keep the fun going. He'd bring out the best in everybody. He'd also be desperate for you to come home and he'd be delighted when you'd arrive. Dogs are like children – their concept of time is different from ours. They'd be longing for you and waiting for you. You wouldn't get that in a person; they'd get bored. So, when you'd arrive, he'd be so happy to see you that he'd run around the table in a circle.

His big weakness was food. He was always waiting for the fridge door to open. He'd be right at my ankles, thinking, 'This is my chance to get some ham or turkey.' He would sit and, if you weren't noticing him, he would do a few quiet barks. He would do anything to get food. That was his big passion in life. Although he was always a wee bit overweight, he carried it very well.

We once went to an agricultural show and decided to enter Bertie and Gypsy in some competitions. Gypsy came second and fifth in two separate categories. Bertie, on the other hand, was just so excited meeting all these different characters – all the different people and other dogs. We decided, therefore, to enter him in The Best of the Worst competition. He came first and ended up having a 'first' rosette hanging off his collar. We were delighted.

Bertie eventually died of kidney failure. We had taken him to the vet's and they were automatically preparing us for the worst. I would have done anything to save him. I asked them to phone other places to see if there was any hope. I even asked for dialysis, which they provide in America. I also prayed for him and I hoped he'd get well, but the prognosis was poor.

On the week he died, he was being kept in the vet's. I'd phone them every morning, at nine o'clock, and I'd ask if they would hold on until noon. Then I'd phone again and I'd ask them to see what he would be like at two o'clock. I kept begging. In midweek, there was a tiny improvement, but the next day we were called in and told, 'He is going to slip into a coma. The last act of kindness you can do is to say goodbye.'

He died in May 2015. I think animals are sent to us by God but he takes them back off us again. To have him was the best thing that ever happened. He was a great friend, companion, co-walker, co-pilot and a very gentle soul. He really was like a diamond shining in a coalmine. It was no surprise that shortly before he died he was licking my hand, just like the gentleman he was. He always had a bit extra. Whatever it is, he had it.

**ÁINE KEANE tells how three pet animals – two dogs and a cat – lit up her life after she got married.**

When we got married and moved into our own house, we got two dogs from the same litter. We were only supposed to be getting one. The second was supposed to be for my husband's friend, but he was away on holidays. The guy we were getting them from said that the mother wasn't able for them, so we took the second dog to mind him. I fell in love with him, and that was the end of him going anywhere else.

Bailey was my dog; Geordi was my husband's. Their dad was a St. Bernard and the mum was a Golden Retriever. They were born in June 2000, so they were our millennium babies. The guy we got them from said they'd be about the same size as a collie, but they turned out to be a lot bigger than any collie I ever saw!

Because they were brothers, they were very close. They slept together and their paws would always be touching. They would eat together. You couldn't take one for a walk and not the other. Wherever one went, the other had to be there, too. When we took one to be groomed, the other would have to sit and watch. Otherwise, they would cry and cry and cry.

We took them to fun dog shows. Bailey was the prize-winner of the two. On one occasion, at a show, my husband decided to take Geordi back to the car. Bailey saw him leaving and pulled me across the fields, through the crowds. There was no stopping him. You just could not separate them.

I eventually got pregnant and I was worried that the two dogs might become jealous. The opposite happened. Bailey would lie on the settee with me, with his head on the bump, listening to the heartbeat. Geordi would be lying on the floor because Bailey, who was very protective, would push him away.

We had a cat at the time, too. We called the cat Sylvester. She was there since before the dogs arrived. When we got her, she was a lovely long-haired black kitten. After a few weeks, my sister-in-law had her up on her lap and she noticed that she wasn't a male. She immediately became Sylvia.

Although she was very jealous when we first got the dogs – tearing curtains and jumping up on the table and regurgitating food while we were eating – she eventually got the message that they were staying. After that, she got on well with them.

She would eat with them, but she was bossy so when she went to the bowl they'd stand back and let her eat first. She also shared their house; we had a special house with a proper slate roof, PVC window, block walls, and non-slip tiles on the floor. It also had a heater on timer. She used to sleep in there with them.

We had cuddly toys for Geordi, who loved them, but Bailey never took to them. The cat used to have play-mice, but Geordie was inclined to swallow them and we'd find chewed-up mice in his poo in the back garden. He did a great job processing them! Bailey was above all that; he was more mature.

On the weekends, when I'd be having a lie-in, they'd arrive up the stairs in the morning and come into the bed with me. All three would be there. They'd sleep on top of the blankets. We'd have a lie-in together.

The three of them also followed me everywhere. If I was sitting on the couch, I'd have three pairs of eyes on me. The minute I'd get up, they'd all stand up. Bailey would be first – he was the pack leader – and Geordi would follow him. They'd line up, with Sylvia taking up position at the rear. She was clever to do that as Geordi ended up weighing nine stone and Bailey eight stone and she didn't want to get trampled on.

We were just like a procession. I might only be going to the kitchen or to the front door to let somebody in. I might be going anywhere. I couldn't go to the toilet without them following me. They wouldn't do it with my husband as Bailey, the leader, would only follow me. The others would then follow him.

I would walk them on the main road, without leads, and they would follow me. If they got a bit far ahead, they would look back to make sure I was following them; if I wasn't, they'd come back. There would be all three of them, with Bailey at the front and the cat at the rear. It would be the same if I took them to the beach, although I would only bring the two dogs there. People thought I was most odd.

Tragedy struck on 20 December 2003. Bailey broke his leg in a freak accident. It was my husband's birthday and we were going out. I left him out the back to do a pee. There were some loose stones there and he fell and badly broke his leg. It was a compound fracture. He was never really right after that; he wasn't himself. About a year later, he started fading before my eyes and was diagnosed with chronic kidney failure. He died, aged less than five, in March 2005.

By that stage, Sylvia had been knocked down and killed. Geordi was very upset by everything that had happened. After Bailey died, he would go running around the house, checking all the rooms to see where he was. He wouldn't even go out for a pee without my standing beside him. We eventually got another dog to keep him company.

Geordi lived a very long and very happy life. He lived until he was 13, which is old for his type of dog, and he was very healthy. We had a birthday party for his tenth birthday. We had a bouncy castle and a cake with his picture on it. I sent out printed invitations. My animal-loving friends turned up, along with their pets. We had a great day. Geordi died a week after his thirteenth birthday, in 2013.

In time, we got new cats and dogs and continued the old traditions, but it was never really the same. The dogs we have now are lovely, but you don't get the same level of loyalty from them. They are very different. They are more independent and aloof. The others were definitely more affectionate.

I currently have three dogs and seven cats. The three dogs weigh 11 stone, nine stone and eight-and-a-half stone. They are big. I still walk down the street with a procession of them behind me. The dogs are there and maybe a cat, too. But nothing will ever be the same as with Bailey, Geordi and Sylvia. I was very lucky to have them. It was very special, and it's never going to happen again.

SEÁN MC CAUL **describes how a dog named Kaiser became the best friend he ever had.**

In December 1998, I bought an Alsatian with the intention of giving it to my daughter as a pet. He was the most beautiful dog you could ever see, just three months old, and coloured black and tan. He was like a big pup. Unfortunately, she didn't have the time to look after him. Although I was never really a lover of dogs, I decided to keep him. It was the best thing that ever happened to me in my life.

We became unbelievably close, just like brothers. We went everywhere together, seven days a week. We would get up at six o'clock every day in the summertime and head for the beach in the car. He would lean over from the back seat and put his head on my shoulder. People used to be looking at us passing by and they would smile or laugh. You could see them pointing at us. If he didn't have his head on my shoulder, it would be out the car window.

Kaiser became just like one of the family. When he was a pup, he would always lie at my feet. When he got older, he would lie beside me on the couch. He would look up at me. We would go shopping together. He slept on the bed. When he was going for a sleep, he would give me a kiss on the cheek. If he saw me lying down to get some sleep, he would give me a kiss on the cheek, too. It was just the kind of dog he was.

He loved going to the beach and he loved the water. When he got out of the car, he would head straight to the sea and splash about. I would towel him off and he would play on the sand. He would chase a ball or some stones. After that, we would come home. When we arrived back at the house, the first thing he would do, yet again, is give me a kiss on the cheek.

When we went for walks over fields, he would lead the way. If we came to a barbed-wire fence, I might need to crawl under it. He wouldn't move until I was safe and standing up again. He looked after me and always made sure I was OK.

He was able to read my mind. He always knew what I was going to do before I did it. If I was thinking of going to the shore, he would be up on his feet, at the door, and ready to go. If I was away somewhere, he would get up and lie at the front door because he knew I would soon be arriving. Every night, when I'd come home from work, he'd be waiting for me. We developed a bond; it was quite unbelievable.

Although I didn't know it at the time, I became known as 'the man with the dog.' We had a special thing going. I remember someone once said, 'That dog idolises you. I know that by the way he looks at you.' The only thing he didn't like was if I had a drink, even a beer. When I'd come home, he'd be raging. He'd give me bad looks. It was like he was saying, 'You shouldn't be drinking!'

My wife and I went on a cruise around March 2000, about 15 months after we got him. I was always talking about going on one. But what happened? I literally cried every night for the dog. I missed him so much. I would phone home at every port we went into to see how he was. The family told me lies. They would say he was fine. I found out later that he would lie in the corner and wouldn't eat. He wouldn't wash, either.

When I came back home, I thought that he would go mad with excitement and jump right up onto me. It didn't happen that way. Instead, he would just lie quietly in the corner. I wondered what was wrong. A vet told me afterwards that dogs blame themselves if you go away. The vet also told me that if I hadn't come back he would have died, he was so brokenhearted. It all worked out fine, though, and we became pals again.

Kaiser had an accident once. I had pulled into a lay-by and we didn't know there was a drop of about 12 feet on the other side of a wall. He dived over the wall and landed on rocks. He was badly hurt, especially in his spine. It broke my heart. I cried for him every day. I was so upset that I couldn't even get out of bed. But we got him well again and all was OK.

Eventually, we had to get him put down. We put him down when he was about eight years of age. We had to because his legs were completely gone. There's a flaw in some dogs, where the rear legs go. He had that flaw, too. It broke my heart. It affected me more than the death of my parents. They died when I was in my 20s. I was in my 60s when Kaiser died and I'll never get over it. His loss was far worse.

I buried him in the garden at home. I have a standing stone outside of our house and I have Kaiser's name on it. There are photographs of him all over the place. Even though he is gone many years now, I still talk about him every day. I could cry about him all day long. He was a heartbreaker, so affectionate, with a beautiful temperament, just like a child. I'll never forget him. He was a great, great, great dog, the best pal I ever had. I'll never, ever get over him.

**Patricia Roche remembers how Bonnie, her eldest Pug, displayed grandmotherly love.**

We have three dogs and they are all Pugs. There's a granny, a mummy and a baby. They are named after characters in *Gone with the Wind*. We got the first, Bonnie, who is the granny, in 2006. Then there's Prissy, who is the daughter and was bred in 2009. Lastly, there's Mellie, who is the granddaughter and was bred in 2014.

I have to cook for them every night. Bonnie loves her food. There's nothing she loves better than a hot curry. She eats hot chillies and also hot peppers. The others love chicken or mince. They understand their food and wouldn't eat it if you didn't give them what they like. They are loveable dogs and I don't mind doing the cooking.

This story is about Bonnie and what happened when her grandchildren were born in 2014. We had to take Prissy to the vet because there were complications and she ended up having a Caesarean section. We were worried that when we brought her pups home, Bonnie might attack them. We thought that she might kill them.

Three pups were born but one of them passed away having lived only a day. We brought the other two home. That morning, we locked Bonnie out in the shed. She was literally throwing herself at the door and she wouldn't eat her breakfast. She kept throwing herself and making noise. It was clear she wanted to come in. By this stage, we realised that she only wanted to see her grandchildren, so we let her inside.

Once she got in, she pushed Prissy out of the way. She just took over. She became like a surrogate mother to the pups. She would keep licking them and cleaning them. She would make sure that they wouldn't fall out of the basket. She put them underneath her to keep them warm. She wouldn't interfere with the feeding; she let the mom do that. When they got a bit bigger and tried to wander away, she would bring them back. She was amazing.

Prissy didn't resent what was happening. She had stitches and had to go back and forth to the vet. She let Bonnie mind the pups. We used to cry just to see what was happening. People used to come to see how she was taking care of them. I think none of us realised that that sort of grandparent thing is also in animals.

What happened gave our Bonnie a new lease of life. At that stage, she was eight years old and had put on a bit of weight. She hadn't been interested in much apart from her food. She was sitting around and lying around. Instead of being a lazy old dog, she now had something to live for. She had a focus.

Eventually, we sold one of the two pups but we kept Mellie. We wanted to keep the generations going. So we now have the three of them, all three generations, and they all have their own personalities. They play together and Bonnie runs up and down the garden with them.

Bonnie hasn't a bad bone in her body. Not many animals do. There's no spite in them, like there might be in humans.

There certainly isn't any in Bonnie. She's a very dear creature, and it is such an endearing story. There we were thinking she was going to do something awful to the pups, but she took them under her wing.

**Jodie recalls an eventful Christmas with Buddy, who was one of her favourite dogs.**

Just after we were married, we got a dog called Buddy. He was our very first dog as a couple together. He was a mix, black and white, and was very like a Jack Russell. He came from a dog belonging to my father-in-law. This was a long time ago, in the late 1970s, and we had only recently moved into our new home.

The first year after we were married, we had Christmas with my family. The second year, we had Christmas on our own. I put in a big effort. I put up a stocking for Buddy, with some dog biscuits and chewy bones. I made a Christmas cake. I made a pudding in a cloth, which I boiled. I cooked a turkey and ham. I had the table set with serviettes and candles. I put out all the glassware that we got as wedding presents. I was delighted with myself.

It was also the very first time I had made a sherry trifle. I remember putting the jam in the sponge and putting the sherry over it. We never put jelly in our trifle; we just used custard with cream on top. I'm afraid I got a bit lavish with the sherry. Before that, at home, my mother would have been in charge of the sherry, but I thought I had done a fabulous job.

Because it was Christmas, I was giving portions of turkey and gravy to the dog and spoiling him. I had wanted him to have something special. He was roaming around the kitchen and sitting by the fire and looking at all that was going on. He was also looking for food.

Without thinking, I gave him some of the trifle. I didn't eat all of mine because it was a bit strong, so I put some of it down for him and he certainly enjoyed it. He lapped it up. He was looking at me as if he was saying, 'Where's the rest of it?' He nearly ate the pattern off his bowl.

He slept for a week afterwards. Oh, the snores off him! You really would want to have heard the snoring! Initially, I thought he had just had a big dinner and he was having a snooze. But then, when he snored, I realised it was different. I nearly died with the fright.

When he properly woke up, he looked like he had a headache and a hangover. He probably did! When he started to walk, he was tottering a bit. He kept looking at me with these doleful eyes. I wondered, 'What have I done to him?' I thought I had killed him.

He looked so sorrowful; for me, it was like a guilt trip with a return ticket. I kept talking to him and giving him drinks. I mentioned it to my father and he couldn't contain himself with the laughing. He said, 'He's OK! He'll be fine!' He thought it was all so funny, and he felt it would all be resolved in time.

Eventually, I gave Buddy half an aspirin. I chopped it up and put it into some jam so he would swallow it. I also gave him lots of water. He was grand after that; there wasn't a bother on him and the aspirin clearly worked. I think, at the end, what happened had a greater effect on me than him!

He turned out to be a very funny dog. My husband, at one time, worked in a very sweaty job. He was so sweaty that when he'd take off his shoes after coming home from work, the tears would sometimes run down my face. It would be especially bad when he'd come in and take his shoes off by the fire.

One day, he came home and sat down on the armchair by the fire and took off his shoes. Buddy was sitting nearby. He looked up at my husband and it seemed like he suddenly went cross-eyed. He fell over in what looked like a faint and just lay there. He went over like a log. Then he got up and walked away. The smell overcame him.

Buddy also hated mice. He was terrified of them, probably more than me. I remember, one day, he was having his dinner outside. Next thing, I heard a screech. I opened the back door and found that there was a mouse in Buddy's kennel. Needless to say, I didn't run after the mouse, either. There was a pair of us in it!

Buddy didn't have any more sherry trifles at Christmas, and I wouldn't advise anyone to do what I did. It's hard to believe what happened because I was even careful not to give him ham because of the salt. But it never crossed my mind for a minute that the sherry could do him harm.

Partly because of Buddy, that first Christmas on our own was a very special time for us. We'll never forget it, just like we'll never forget our son's first Christmas. We still have the dinner service and the canteen of cutlery that we used that day. Unfortunately, we don't have Buddy; he eventually died in his sleep from old age. But I still remember him as a lovely dog. He always looked after me and was the best of company for me for as long as he lived.

**PATRICIA explains what her dog Poppy did at the time when a neighbour unexpectedly died.**

My daughter used to own a dog which she got from the pound in Dublin. Her name is Poppy and she is a cross between a collie and an Alsatian, we think. She is pure black and would remind you of a Labrador. The problem in Dublin was that she had no place to run around apart from the garden of my daughter's house, and she made a dreadful mess of it. On one occasion, we brought her to Kerry with the intention that she would stay a couple of weeks while the grass grew in Dublin. But once she came to Kerry, I think she had no intention of going back to Dublin.

She quickly became a part of the family. She has her own home out the back, where she has a bed. It's beside the garage, in a shed for turf and coal and timber and things like that. It's her private home. We also have a lot of land around where we live, so she has great freedom. In the summer she is out all the time but we allow her in during the winter. She especially loves going to the beach and every time she goes she has to bring a stone home with her.

She is such a bright dog, very intelligent. She always knows when we are about to take her for a walk. She scratches the patio door, comes into the kitchen and makes six circles around it, as if asking, 'Are you ready yet?' Although she can't open the patio door, she can open the one into the kitchen and that's how she often enters to see if we are ready.

She loves going for a drive in the car. We always put her in the front seat, sitting on a big bath towel, looking out the window. My husband drives, she's in the passenger seat and I'm in the back. Our neighbour sometimes drives her in his car, where she's also in the front. He has trained her to put her paw in his hand in case she becomes afraid. He also puts the radio on for her. We do the same in our own car. A person we know, having seen Poppy sitting up in the front of the car, once said, 'I've seen it all now!'

Our neighbour's daughter has special needs. Poppy is unreal with her. They sit beside each other. The daughter will feed her, give her water and sit with her arms around her. Poppy is very protective and loves to be with her. If the daughter comes to our house, the dog will scratch at the door until we let her in. She will then come in, sit down beside the daughter and look up at her, yawning and doing things like that.

There was a woman from Dublin who used to come down and stay in a holiday home near us. She was in her late 70s. I had never met her and I didn't know her, but our Poppy did. Sometimes, when this woman would pass our house to go for a walk, Poppy would join her. They might walk to the nearby pier.

One evening, I saw her going to the pier and Poppy was with her. It was in summertime, around seven o'clock. I was in the sitting-room and could see them together. On their way back, I saw them again. I thought the woman was probably heading home and Poppy would soon come back.

After a while, however, I heard a dog barking. As it happened, another neighbour was going for a walk and he heard a dog barking, too. He thought, 'That's strange. I wonder what it's barking at.' He went off down the road. My husband headed down, too, to see what the barking was all about. It was Poppy and she was barking for all she was worth, standing upright with her head up in the air.

Next to Poppy was the woman, who was lying down on the ground, in the middle of the road, and she was dead. The poor woman had got a heart attack. Poppy had obviously stayed with her, standing right beside her, howling for all she was worth. She was obviously trying to attract help while staying with the woman. My husband tried to get Poppy to come home, but she wouldn't move; she wanted to stay there.

We eventually brought Poppy home and fed her and put her in her shed. We stayed with her for the rest of the evening. It was clear that she knew something had gone on and that the woman had fallen down. She was obviously with the woman as she passed away. She needed the attention and she eventually settled down, but it was clear that she knew something had happened and that she sensed something was wrong.

Without Poppy's barking, who knows what might have happened? It was a very small country road. It was getting towards dusk. Maybe a car would have gone down the road bringing someone to feed their animals. They mightn't have seen the woman in the road and could have rolled over her. Otherwise, I don't think anyone would have gone by. The barking, which wasn't at all like Poppy, was what drew our attention to what happened.

To this day, Poppy won't leave me, possibly because of what took place. I can't go anywhere on my own. She accompanies me wherever I go. She is my bodyguard and a sort of guard dog. When I'm out walking with her and she rambles off into a field, I shout out her name and she's back immediately. Even if I stop to tie my shoelace, she's back straightaway.

If we go somewhere in the car for shopping and she can't come with us, we say to her, 'Mind the house! Mind the house!' She will sit there and will still be sitting there when we come back. She has taken on a big minding role and is very protective of us and the house. We always feel safer with her there. She really takes care of us.

Poppy is such a pleasant dog. She is nice to people and has a brilliant personality. She is always good. She wouldn't attack anything; if she saw a cow, she'd run from it. But ever since that day the woman died, she really minds us. Even if the people with the special needs daughter go away, she will sit by their door until they come back. She is wonderful and beautiful. We never intended to have a dog, but this is what we got, and that's what happened.

**RITA reminisces about Becky, her close companion and a great source of fun and affection.**

My dog was a mixed breed, half terrier and half sheepdog. She was white and brown and had a lovely nature. Her name was Becky. She was advertised in a paper and my husband's niece got her. She had two other dogs, both of them big, so she asked me if I would take her. I said, 'No, I don't want a dog.' My niece then asked me could she leave her with me when she was in town. Becky never left from that day on.

I was living alone. My husband had died years earlier from a stroke. I was on my own after that. I used to have another dog but she was an old stray dog and she died a few months after Becky arrived. From then on, I just had Becky. She always wanted to be with me. She was happy and was great company.

She soon knew my every move. She would watch TV with me, and she particularly liked seeing other animals. When the *Fair City* opening tune came on, she'd wake up because she could see a dog featured at the start. She'd go down to the TV until the dog was gone; then she'd come back up and lie down again.

In the summertime, when Gaelic football matches would be on TV, I might clap if someone scored a point. She would hear me doing it and she would then go down to her basket and pull out a ball. There was one particular ball she liked, which was red, and she'd bring it up and put it on my lap as if to say, 'Play with me!'

If visitors came in, she'd make them welcome but she was only happy as long as they didn't overstay. If it was near her feeding time, between half past five and six, she'd want them to go. She'd stand in front of them and bark and come over to me as if to say, 'It's time to feed me!' People would know she wanted them gone.

If she thought I was going someplace where she couldn't go – like to Mass – the moment she would see me with the car keys or changing my shoes, she'd go down to the room and go under the bed. Alternatively, she might go out and lie under the car so that I couldn't move it. I would have to pull her out from under it or open up the boot and she would jump in. I had a hatchback and she could see out.

She loved shoes. If I was going out on my own, I might leave her in the outhouse. She would be very happy when I'd arrive back home. I had a couple of pairs of shoes out there and she'd be waiting for me with a shoe. She would bring the shoe into the house in her mouth. She'd leave it in the middle of the floor.

If she thought there was someone at the door when I was out, she'd come to the door with a shoe in her mouth. If the person went away, she'd drop the shoe at the door and head back to her bed. If another person arrived, she'd bring down another shoe. She always had to have something for them. I'd know how many people called while I was out by the number of shoes at the door.

She loved going for walks. I would walk her for about half a mile and I might do that a few times a day. When we were coming home and turning into the house, if she didn't want to come in she would pull me across to the other side of the road. We would have to go further. She was the boss!

I also used to take her to terrier racing and she would always win. The races were held at carnivals and race meetings in a field. The owners would go up to the finishing point and the dogs would be down at the other end. Then we'd call them. She ended up with five or six plaques.

She actually won one race three years in a row. I also took her to dog shows, where she got first once and also got a few seconds. A vet once said she deserved a prize for barking alone; she was always barking at the other dogs!

She died in 2014, aged 14. She had got old and she died as a result of a cruciate ligament injury. Her cruciate just went. I brought her to the vet and they operated. They thought she was strong enough to survive but she just faded away.

I missed her for ages, for 12 months or more. The place was empty without her. She had been wonderful company. Wherever I was, she was there. Without her, I was lonely. I always knew she was important to me but her death brought it home. She was a lovely dog and I still wish she was here.

**TONY HERBERT remembers a bossy but beautiful Yorkshire Terrier called Eppie.**

Eppie was a Yorkie and was the boss of the house. When we got her, she was tiny; you could hold her in the palm of your hand. She was coloured black and brown and was very attached to my wife Kay. When Kay went to buy her, there were three or four puppies there. Eppie came up onto Kay's lap straightaway.

The woman who was selling the puppies was very fussy and said to Kay, 'You'll have to pay me two or three visits before I'll give you the dog.' She was wondering if Kay was only buying her for breeding or something like that. But Kay proved herself and Eppie arrived home.

She became very protective of Kay. When Kay would be sitting on the settee, no one else could sit there. Eppie would be lying up against Kay, with her back to her and watching everything. Kay might ask one of us, 'Could you give me my handbag,' but you couldn't touch it, not a hope in hell. She'd protect the handbag straightaway.

She slept with the two of us. She would get into my side of the bed and wouldn't leave me in. I'd say to Kay, 'I can't get into the bed!' Kay would reply, 'Don't be disturbing the dog!' I'd have to try and sneak in. She really was Kay's dog and just tolerated the rest of us.

She had a favourite teddy bear and would bring it with her to bed. It was just a normal brown teddy bear that had belonged to one of the lads. She loved it and took it over. She dragged it around with her and would cuddle into it in bed. If you tried to take it from her, your hand would be gone.

She really thought she owned the place and was watching all the time. She'd watch everything you were doing. She'd follow me if I went up to the attic. About two or three seconds before the doorbell would ring, she would know someone was coming and would be up and out of her chair.

She always was the first to be served food. She loved chicken. I might come in from work at half past five, but who would be served first? Eppie! The rest of us would be sitting around the table waiting for our dinner, but Eppie would be chewing away on the floor from her bowl. She knew her place in the house – number one!

She was a fabulous dog and was so intelligent. I had a very bad accident and I had to sit in an electrified reclining chair; if I sat on a couch, I would hardly have been able to get out of it again. Eppie developed the habit of sitting on the left side of the chair so she could look out the window. She would do that with her head between her paws. If anyone came in the gate, she would start barking straightaway. To this day, when I sit on the chair, I sit on the other side and leave the left side for Eppie.

I ended up lying flat in bed. Kay would lie down on the floor and Eppie would lie down alongside her. If I moved in any way, Eppie would jump up. She would then attract Kay's attention to make sure she was looking after me. If Kay was asleep and I started moving or moaning with the pain, she'd lick Kay's face, telling her to wake up.

I nearly killed her once. I came home from work in the very early hours of the morning. I arrived into the kitchen and I didn't turn on the light. Next thing, in the darkness, I saw this black thing running across the floor. I thought it was a rat. It went in under the table, so I got the brush. I suddenly realised it was Eppie. Thankfully, I realised it was her just in time.

On a further occasion, I got soaked because of Eppie. We took her to the beach and all of a sudden she started barking out at the sea. She then went straight into the water and started swimming. We were calling but she wasn't turning back. In the end, I had to run in, fully clothed, and swim out after her. I'm not a great swimmer but I had no choice. I got her to turn around and come back in. I don't know why she did it; all I know is that I got soaking wet and had to go home.

After my father died, we inherited Sooty, his dog. When he was dying, he asked us to take him over. He was a lovely dog, a West Highland Terrier, but Eppie barely tolerated him. She'd bark at Sooty and growl at him if he came in around the dining-room or sitting-room.

The poor old dog was restricted to the kitchen. We had to put a baby gate across the door from the kitchen out into the dining-room. Sooty would be outside looking in, while Eppie would be stretched out on the settee. She would be glancing at him to see what he'd be getting up to.

The two of them were together for about four years. One of my memories is of them waiting at the gate for me to come home from work. They would know by the sound when I was on my way. They'd be jumping up and down. If I was having a bad day at work, they'd cheer me up when I came home. They'd be looking up at me to take them for a walk. I could read their eyes.

They were both so lovely that they'd make you wonder at the things people do to animals. You'd wonder about the cruelty they inflict on them – on dogs and donkeys and lots of other creatures. Good Lord, you'd wonder what's going through people's minds. The pain and suffering that they inflict! These animals are so beautiful, and all they want is love and affection.

Sooty died first and we had him cremated. We kept his ashes in the house for ages. Eppie lived longer, until she was 12, but she got cancer. Kay had to take her down to put her to sleep. I think she knew what was happening because she licked Kay's hand and then put her head down and went to sleep.

We brought her home and put her in a box and buried her at the end of the garden. It was like there was a death in the family. We buried Sooty's ashes with her. We put Eppie's teddy bear in the box, and also Sooty's blanket. Everybody was sitting around crying because everybody knew Eppie. Even the neighbours came in and they were crying. Kay was in convulsions, of course. But it was the kindest thing to do, to put her to sleep.

They were both beautiful dogs but Eppie stood out mainly for the love she showed for Kay. She loved the rest of us but, to Eppie, Kay was special. We still miss her around the place. We still talk about her and have her pictures around the house. She was living proof that if you give a dog love, the dog will return it tenfold.

# CAT TAILS

American author Mark Twain adored cats. He could not live without them. He called his cats Sour Mash, Abner, Beelzebub, Zoroaster, Bambino, among many other names. He loved their sense of playfulness and fun. One would snuggle in a corner pocket of his billiard table and change the direction of passing balls with his paw.

Others, named Sackcloth and Ashes, would weep when he recited German, 'frantically give thanks' when he recited French, and walk away when he sang. They were also independent, as exemplified by Sour Mash, who didn't 'give a damn' about other people's opinions.

We may think that we comprehend cats, but if you really understood the language they use in fights it would 'give you the lockjaw,' Mark Twain concluded. This sense of independence, fun and intelligence, so well articulated by Mark Twain, is evident in many of the following stories.

**CONOR CLANCY recollects how his cat Chester undertook an adventure that ended up on TV.**

Chester is a stray cat who was taken in by a friend of ours. He was part of a litter of four kittens. We took one and they kept the rest. He is black and white, with black spots around his eyes and black spots on his nose. He was about six or seven weeks old when we got him, and he is very cute.

From the beginning, he was very inquisitive and fearless, with no sense of self-preservation. He would try to do things that would almost give you a heart attack and that other cats would never do because they would be too smart. For example, he would jump to catch flies but he'd flip himself over when he'd jump and he'd land on his back really hard. We'd look at him and think, 'Oh, no! He's just broken his back!' Then he'd get up and do it again.

He'd also climb a tall tree out the back. It's an elder tree. From day one, he'd climb up to the top of it. You could see his eyes following the trunk upwards and he'd be thinking, 'My God! I can climb that!' So he'd go straight up and would stand there. You'd see this little kitten right on top of the tree. He always had a great sense of adventure. But he's not stupid; he's just fearless.

We only had him about two weeks when he went missing. My partner Nyree and our son Tom had gone to New Zealand on holidays. They had gone about a week. One night, I was leaving the house to go to a music rehearsal. Chester had been out in the back garden, so before I left I made sure he was brought inside. I closed all the windows and doors. He was definitely inside the house before I left. I then went out the front door and I caught my bus.

A few hours later, I came back and I couldn't see Chester. That wasn't too unusual because Chester might have been off somewhere asleep. I had a stroll around but couldn't find him. After about ten minutes, I started to get worried. I wondered if he had crawled into some nook or cranny and got stuck. I kept calling him and I was getting very concerned. I couldn't hear him crying out. I tried everywhere, inside and out. This was now two o'clock in the morning and panic was setting in. I was getting very upset.

The next day, I made up flyers asking if anyone had seen Chester and I put them into letterboxes up and down my street. I talked to my next-door neighbour and he was asking around, as well. I didn't call my partner in New Zealand because I didn't want to upset her. A previous cat of ours had died not long before, so the news would have been awful. The whole day passed by and that night I stayed at the computer because I couldn't sleep.

At about two o'clock in the morning, I got a text from someone whose number I didn't recognise. It said, 'I just saw a cat on the RTÉ website. It could be your cat.' I rushed onto the website and there was this video of a cat stuck in the middle of the M50 motorway. They had a video taken by someone from the DSPCA. The news story just said, 'Kitten rescued on M50. Traffic stopped.' I really wasn't sure it was him, so I rang the DSPCA and left a message. They got back to me first thing in the morning.

That morning, I went out to the DSPCA, in Rathfarnham, and there was Chester! I was so delighted it was him. I recognised him the moment I saw him. I recognised his distinct markings, especially on his stomach, which hadn't been clear on the video. But while I was delighted and happy, he was totally nonplussed by my presence. He had a look on his face that said, 'Oh! That's the person who feeds me sometimes!' He was indifferent. He just looked at me and went off and did something else.

They told me how Chester had been found in the middle of the M50, near Dundrum. He was crouched down beside one of the concrete barriers, with the traffic whizzing by and no way to escape. Someone reported it. When the woman from the DSPCA got to him, she thought he was dead because he wasn't moving. But she noticed that he sort of shivered every time a car went by, so she wondered if he was alive. She couldn't get across to him because the motorway was so busy, so she had to call the guards to stop the traffic.

What was amazing was that we live about 15 miles away from Dundrum, where he had been found. It would have been impossible for Chester to have made it out there all by himself, especially as he was picked up within 12 hours of leaving our house. The lady from the DSPCA said that it's not unheard of for cats to climb up through the axles of a car, into the engine block, and sit on top of a warm engine. It's also not unusual for someone to get in and drive away while the cat is still in there.

What Chester probably did was he sneaked out of the house as I left. He is cunning and fast. As I went out the front door, he must have run out and I didn't see him. He must have then jumped up into a car. Eventually, he must have fallen out of the engine block and then ended up on the M50. That's what they figured had happened.

An RTÉ camera crew was at the DSPCA and they filmed me being united with Chester. A reporter from one of the tabloids interviewed me, as well. Photographs were taken. Other papers rang me during the day. I was also interviewed by Dave Fanning on radio. When my partner came back from her holiday, she went into her workplace and everybody knew about what had happened.

There was even a guy who used to work with me some years ago who messaged me on Facebook to say that he was living in Vancouver and he saw it on the news there. I went into a bar and the barman offered me a free pint because of Chester. I was also walking down one of the Dublin quays about a week later and a taxi was driving past me. The taxi driver leaned out the window and roared, 'How's your cat?'

As for Chester, I brought him home and it was like he had never been away. He had some food and a little snooze. He chased some flies. And he was fine. It was as if nothing had ever happened to him. But he didn't change. Only yesterday, he got up on top of our garage and started heading off over a terrace of garages lined up in a row. No matter how much I called, he kept going.

When he eventually decided to come back, I was standing there with my head just above the level of the roof of the garage. As he approached, all he could see was my disembodied head. He freaked out. He puffed out all his fur, made himself bigger and arched his back. Then he realised it wasn't a disembodied head; it was only me behind the garage. He looked at me as if to say, 'Yes? What do you want?'

**PAT O'BRIEN recalls two memorable cats – one attached to his wife, the other attached to him.**

One Christmas Eve, my wife was talking to a friend who lives just down the road. My wife was sitting in the car and her friend was standing out on the footpath. They eventually said goodbye and my wife was ready to go. Suddenly, her friend said, 'Stop! Stop! Stop! There's a little kitten under your front wheel!'

Eleanor got out of the car, picked up the kitten and brought her home. Probably because my wife had picked up the kitten, she became the cat's number-one favourite person. She was a tiny black-and-white kitten, absolutely smashing. We decided to call her Holly on account of it being Christmas.

She turned out to be an amazing cat. Eleanor and I were having an awful row one day. We were sitting on high stools in the kitchen. The cat jumped up on the high stool between the two of us. She rubbed her head off both of us. In other words, she was saying, 'Would you stop?' The two of us just looked at one another and we stopped arguing immediately.

I worked as a baker for a long, long time, so I would work nights and sleep days. As a result, later on, I found it hard to sleep at night. I would often be lying in the sitting-room during the day because I would be tired. Holly would usually come and scratch at the door of the house, trying to get in to lie on my lap. I found it hard to get any sleep when she'd be lying on me, so I would often tell her to go away. And away she'd go.

One particular day, she started scratching at the door and I left a couple of roars at her. It made no difference; she just would not stop scratching. I was furious and I hopped up off the settee. As soon as I opened the door, she flew right into the kitchen. I went in after her to see what all the carry-on was about.

And there, in the kitchen, was the pot on top of the gas stove, the gas was still on, and there were billows of smoke coming out of the pot! Only for her, the house could have gone up in flames. I hugged her and said, 'Thanks very much.' She looked at me as if to say, 'No problem!' She knew what she had done.

Although she was a very independent cat and kept mostly to herself, she was also very inquisitive. If I put up a ladder and went up to the attic, she'd be straight up after me. I'd call her to get her down, but she would dig her nails into me and refuse to move. The only way I could get her down was to put her into a box and carry her. The alternative was to get Eleanor to call her. Eleanor would say, 'Come on, Holly! Come on, love!' and straight down the ladder she'd come.

She would check out everywhere. We have cupboards under the stairway and if you left them half-open she'd be in there like a flash. She also ended up stuck on top of an extension we were building to the house. She had somehow got up there and there was no way she was coming down. All I could do was put on leather gloves to stop her digging her nails into me and up I went to the top of the wall. The trouble I had trying to get her down was unbelievable!

We would let her out, but she wouldn't stay long outside. One day, however, she went out and didn't come back. We looked all over the place and couldn't find her. Four days later, we had to go out and my wife suggested, 'Why don't we leave the window ajar because she might come back?' I agreed reluctantly because of the danger of being robbed. When we came back into the house, there she was meowing at us. She was so excited to see us.

I was downtown a few weeks afterwards and a guy asked me, 'Have you got a black-and-white cat?' 'We have,' I said. He then described the cat and told me, 'She was sitting on my window ledge for four days and every time I'd go near her to help her she'd spit at me.' She wouldn't let anyone go near her except Eleanor or myself. She had obviously gone off on a bit of a safari, to see what was around the next corner, and then possibly couldn't find her way back. She never left the house after that.

I brought another cat home while we still had Holly. I found him lying at the side of the footpath, with cars flying up and down beside him. He was only a tiny furball. I looked at him and said, 'I'm sorry, we have a cat, and one is enough.' I went to my car and was about to get in the door when his little head came up and looked at me. I said, 'Oh, my God! I just can't leave him there!' I caught him and brought him home.

We called him Mister. He was a foxy-coloured cat and he had an amazing walk. When you'd see him walking along the footpath, he was like John Wayne going from side to side. It was a real swagger. Everybody used to remark on it. Because I had picked him up, he was really my cat. While Holly would come to Eleanor, Mister would come to me.

Holly never took to Mister at all. Mister used to tease her all the time. He was a blackguard and spent his time tormenting her. He would grab her tail and hold onto it. The screeching would bring me along and off Mister would go; he'd be gone. It was like he would tease her just to bring her to a high level of temper.

You'd swear to God you could hear Mister laughing as he was running away. He was a total rogue. They never got on. They couldn't stand one another. They each had to have their individual bowls. You could see that Holly wanted to kill him, but we loved them both.

Holly died first. She lived until she was 18 years old. We knew the end was coming because of her age. One night, she walked over and went into the dog's bed. I was about to go into the sitting-room to watch TV but Eleanor said, 'Do you want to say goodbye to the cat in case she's dead by the time you come back?' I said, 'There's no killing that one!'

I went into the sitting-room and sat down. I immediately thought, 'Maybe I should have done what Eleanor suggested.' So I went back in and I knelt down and rubbed her. She lifted up her head and looked straight into my eyes. She held that look for about ten seconds. She then put her head down, and that was the last of Holly.

Mister died not long after. He had an operation for urinary problems and afterwards he wasn't himself. All he wanted to do was go upstairs, into the back bedroom, and lie down. We took him downstairs again and brought him into the sitting-room.

At one stage, Eleanor was sitting beside him on the couch. Suddenly, he hopped off the couch, walked across the floor, and then just dropped down on the floor and died. It was around Christmas and we couldn't get him cremated. We just wrapped him in a blanket and buried him out in the back.

We did have Holly cremated, however, and we kept her ashes. We still have them today. She was unreal. I never realised until she was gone all the things she had done and all the memories she had left behind. But we will never forget either of those cats. They will both be with us forever. They really were very, very special.

**JOHN CORBETT describes his lifelong love of cats, reaching back to when he was a young boy.**

I had 28 cats at one time, up to about ten or 12 years ago. I have three or four acres, so I could look after them. I actually bought four or five wooden houses so they could be warm and safe. I put boxes, newspapers and blankets into the houses. The cats were very cosy and were well-protected from danger or bad weather.

Twenty-eight cats were too many to handle. The numbers grew fast. The cats would go away and have kittens and hide them. They didn't want to bring them back in case I'd give them away or get them put down. Then they'd sneak them back in over time. Through my being so soft-hearted, I kept them all. Eventually, I got them neutered and the numbers gradually fell back down. I have only five now.

I have probably had hundreds of cats over the years – Tom, Rocky, Mini-Moo, Towser and Felix, a long list of them. All of them had different personalities. Some were very standoffish, while others became very close to me. A lot of them were very affectionate and would come and rub up against my leg. They always showed great warmth.

I would only allow one into my house. There was always a special one. My latest is called Mini. She's as clever as you could get, very intelligent. But they were all special in their own way. They know their owners and become very attached to them.

Cats have great cuteness and can read your mind. You know that from the way they look at you and stare at you. They seem to be sizing you up. They can read your personality and can see through you. They know more, and are more intelligent, than we give them credit for.

They are independent animals, with minds of their own. A cat will always do its own thing. That's why they say you own a dog but you never own a cat. You could say, though, that when they want things they can become very close and show great friendship!

You've got to remember that they are free-roaming animals; their wildness goes back to the tiger and cheetah. Initially, they were used for keeping down vermin, such as mice and rats. Then they became domesticated through the years and weren't interested in killing anymore. They are now quite gentle creatures, and that's why you see them in most houses today.

I had one, a few years ago, called Mini-Moo. I had her until she was about 12 years old. She was a mixture of a Persian and an ordinary straight-haired cat. She was very affectionate and was coloured foxy and white. She knew when you were coming and going. She always knew everyone's movements.

She could open the door for you. She would know if someone had gone into a room. She'd cock her ears and go to the door and open it. She'd use her paws. Unfortunately, Mini-Moo got ill and died in 1998. The vets couldn't save her.

Cats come and go, disappear and never return, while some die of diseases ranging from cat flu to leukaemia. I've had some who disappeared for maybe a year. They might go rambling through the fields and live in the wild. After a year or so, they would return looking a bit gaunt. I often think they are living out their animal instincts. However, they are just like a computer and know their way back.

One who disappeared on me was a cat called Felix. He was black and white. Someone left him in to me as a kitten, when he was only about two or three months old. He was genuinely affectionate and could do everything but talk.

He would look in a window and call for me to let him into the house. If I didn't let him in, he'd go over to another window to make sure I had seen him. He would be up on the piers of the gate waiting for me to come home. He knew the sound of the car.

I had him for about three and a half years. He used to walk down to a house by the seaside just to visit. Then, one day, he went away across the beach and I never saw him again. I really do miss him. Losing him was a traumatic experience. That's the way with cats. Maybe a dog or a fox got him. Maybe he was stolen. I just don't know.

Another cat I had would pretend that he didn't notice my movements, but he did. I'd be going down to a nearby house opening the windows for the summer. When I'd be leaving my own home, he'd pretend he didn't see me or notice me moving. When I'd arrive at the other house, he'd jump up on my shoulder. He'd be there. He'd have me in contact all the time.

There's a lot of spirituality about cats, more than we give them credit for. They were revered in ancient Egypt, going back to the time of the Pharaohs. They held a special place in society and were regarded as something to be adored, not to be harmed in any way. The death penalty was imposed on anybody who killed or injured a cat.

There's good reason for that. I think they have a sixth sense. They can tell things very quickly. They mourn the loss of other animals or their owners when they pass away. In that sense, they are just like the honeybee. They say that honeybees always know when there is a death in a house. It was an old custom, in times gone by, that when a member of your family died you'd go to the hive and tell the bees. The older people at that time did that. Cats are like honeybees, too.

I've had cats all my life, from about the age of eight, and I've always had a special time for them. I think you remember your animals in the same way that you remember members of your family; you get so attached to them. I have memories of all of them. I miss them all individually. They really show you a lot of affection and pay you back double. They have all been great.

**PAUD CURRAN explains how the family cat never forgot her owners even after the passage of eight years apart.**

In late 1987, we had been down in County Waterford for the weekend. We were driving back and we saw a sign on a farmer's gate saying, 'Potatoes for sale.' We pulled in to get some, to bring them back to Dublin. We parked in the yard, with our three kids in the back of the car.

There were lots of tiny kittens and cats there, and one of the kittens came over to the car. It was a black ball of fluff. She was meowing into the car. The farmer said, 'If you want the kitten, I have plenty of them so you can take her away. You have to take her; she has picked you out.' That's what we did. We brought her back to Dublin.

We then had to find her a name. She had very long hair on her legs and a long coat. She looked like one of those Russian dancers. That suggested a Russian name. Pushkin came to mind, and because she was female we called her Miss Pushkin. It had a catty sound.

She was a really affectionate cat. Everybody loved her. She would sometimes sleep with the kids, sneaking in and lying on their beds. She would also sleep in the hot-press. If you were sitting and reading the newspaper, she would feel slighted and jump up on top of the paper. She had to make sure you were giving her your full attention.

Before we knew it, she was pregnant. We were moving house at the time. We had a cat having kittens with everything going on. She had the kittens in the old house almost on the very day we were moving. We managed to find a home for all of them. It was a hectic time but we managed, although we eventually had to have her spayed.

By mid-1990, less than three years after we got her, I had to move to Africa. The whole family was moving with me. We anticipated being away for three or four years. The question came up about what we would do with the house and Miss Pushkin. We couldn't take her with us. My sister was looking for a place to stay, so she moved in and agreed to look after the cat.

After the first period was over, I was offered a further four years and I decided to take it, so we were away for the best part of eight years. In all this time, we never went back to the house, even when we were home on holidays. We did get reports about the cat, but we never saw her from the time we left.

Meanwhile, my sister moved out and my nephew moved into the house in Dublin. He was sharing the house with some other people who would be coming and going. One of them had a dog for a short period of time. Possibly because of that, Miss Pushkin suddenly disappeared. She just walked out and never came back.

It was reported to us that the cat was gone, and because she hadn't come back my nephew believed she had been knocked down by a car. We were very upset to hear the news. My wife and I were sad; the kids, too. We accepted that when we got back to Ireland, Miss Pushkin wouldn't be there.

After eight years abroad – and two years after Miss Pushkin had disappeared – my wife and I came home to Ireland. Our two eldest lads, who were now just past their teens, came back about a week before us. The house had been vacant for a couple of weeks and the grass had grown in the back garden.

Within half an hour in the house – they were just in the door – didn't Miss Pushkin emerge from the long grass! She just walked out. She recognised my sons and knew them immediately. They were amazed. They couldn't believe it. They didn't expect to ever see her again. My wife and I were amazed, too, when we heard it. Miss Pushkin had re-entered our lives.

We eventually found out that there was an old lady nearby who had been feeding Miss Pushkin. Apparently, the cat had appeared at her house, where she would get fed and then walk away again. She had to survive somehow. The woman had even taken her to the vet. Otherwise, it seems, she had become a stray.

For the remaining years of her life, Miss Pushkin hardly ever left our house. Even if my wife went down the garden to hang out the clothes, she would go down with her. She also became crazy for food, maybe because of the uncertainty of having no regular supplies for years.

There was one occasion when she had a standoff with a fox over a bowl of food. We heard a screeching sound and I went to the window and said to my wife, 'Quick! Come and look!' She was between the fox and the food, and she won. We also have some marvellous photos of her with her head resting on her food dish while she was asleep and waiting for the next refill!

Looking back, it seems that Miss Pushkin probably felt she couldn't live in the house if there was a dog there, or there were too many people coming and going, and she had simply moved out. She must have been checking things out occasionally to see if we would return. She obviously kept in her head an ongoing association with our family and the house.

Miss Pushkin died about six years later, at the age of 17. She died of old age. She had been the cat of our lives and was special to us. We associated her with the kids growing up and many other events. She really had a strong association with lots of things in our lives. Even after eight years without us, she came back and started all over again. I suppose you could say she came home.

**May Hickey's cat is a mouse-catcher of note but also a most wonderful pet.**

There's nothing Sooty likes better than to bring in a mouse. She loves doing it. She will lay the dead mouse on the mat by the fire so I will see it. There will be a lot of activity until I see the mouse. She feels so proud. I have to say, 'You're a great girl for catching mice!'

I was inside in bed one morning and I saw her coming in the window. I thought, 'Is that something inside her mouth?' It was a mouse. She left it on the mat in front of the fire. Another time, there was wicked activity during the night and she had another mouse killed by the fire in the morning.

I hate mice. I think it's the suddenness of them. You know the way they jump unexpectedly? I hate that, and I hate them. I was telling the vet about her and he said, 'She's a hunter.' I saw her in action once; if she thinks there's a mouse somewhere, she'll stay sitting there until she gets it. When she catches a mouse, she gets it in one second. She's an out-and-out hunter.

We got Sooty in a strange sort of way. My daughter Yvette briefly had a cat. It was a small, delicate kitten she found above in the garden. The poor little fellow looked like he was dying. His mother had abandoned him. She took him to the vet, but there was nothing that could be done for him and he died.

She then rang the vet because she knew they would often be told by people about kittens that would be available. They mentioned a place where we might find one. Off we went to this house and a mother cat was there with eight kittens around her. They were only six weeks old and they were all eating out of a dish.

I knew immediately which cat Yvette would opt for. There were coloured cats, white cats and black-and-white ones there, but I said, 'I bet she'll take the black one!' That's what she did, and we set off to take her home. I had the cat on my lap and Yvette was driving. I said, 'What are you going to call her?' She said, 'I don't know.' I said, 'She's so black, why don't you call her Sooty?' And that's how Sooty was named.

I had cats before – Squeak, Moggy and Silver. My mother had a cat called Felix. I always said I wouldn't have any more, but then Sooty arrived and she's now here nine years. She's completely toilet-trained. She doesn't talk; she doesn't speak. If she's hungry, she squeaks very low. She goes out in the morning and she sits up on the roof outside. She loves lying out in the sun.

She's so clever that at five o'clock every morning during the summer, after I'd open the front window, she'd go out to the shore in the street to do her wee-wee. In wintertime, I wouldn't have the window open, but she will come down to my bedroom, where I might be sound asleep, and she'll sit up on the side of the bed looking at me. That means – toilet!

She won't eat cheap food. All she will eat is Felix, with the vegetables and the carrots. I got other brands, on occasions, when the shop's stock of Felix would be out, but she wouldn't touch them. When I come home from town, I'll have the Felix and the nuts with me. She'll know that I have the new boxes and she'll go running in and out under my legs.

I might have some Felix left in an old box, but that's no good. I'll have to open the new box and take out a new pack. She'll be so excited that she'll almost knock me over. I'll have to say, 'Mind, you'll knock me!' But she'll continue to go running in and out under my legs.

I think Sooty is great. She always sits by the fire in the winter. I open the stove and she loves the heat. In the summer, she sits on the chair over by the window. She won't go out if it's raining. If she does go out, and I'm trying to find her, I just stand at the back door and shake the box of nuts and she will come running back inside.

My husband likes her, too, even though he has no time for cats. But he's mad about Sooty. She'll come in and sit up beside him. He'll look at her and say, 'You're here a long time now, Sooty' and he'll give her a pet.

She loved our former dog, Bell. They were best friends and were together a long time. Bell might be with me at work for the day. When I'd come home, Sooty would run over and stroke her head up against Bell and rub against her and show she was delighted to see her.

After Bell died, however, she would sit at a window and look down at her grave out the back. She might, instead, go to where Bell is buried and sit there the whole time. She will sometimes go to the grave and roll on top of it. I think cats know what goes on.

She really is great company and terrific fun. I'd be here at night and Sooty would be up on the chair on one side and Tiny, my dog, would be on the other side. She likes her treats and likes her crisps. I'd never be without her. She really is a beautiful, clever cat, even if she has a liking for mice!

**MAGGIE HEARNE has had a menagerie of cats, each of them lovable, although one, named Bats, stood out from the rest.**

I am very close to cats and have had lots of them over the years. I had 28 at one stage and I kept them outside, but when the number got smaller I brought them in. It all began when two cats wandered into my garden. I called them Tommy Duttons and Chubby. I looked after them and fed them, and I did everything for them. That was in the 1980s.

Tommy Duttons was the first to arrive. I can't explain where the name came from; it just seemed to fit even though the cat was a she. She used to lick my husband Martin's head every evening when he'd come in from work. She'd lick his head from top to bottom. She was also particular about what she ate; she wouldn't touch my burgers, only those from Supermac's.

Chubby, who was next, was a beautiful cat and a little bit overweight, so that's how she got her name. She used to throw herself all over the place. Chubby would lie on the floor, come in the window, go out the window, travel off and come back. I'd give her a bit of corned beef and she'd love it. When I'd come back from the shopping, she'd be jumping in the window for the corned beef and the ham.

They started expanding quickly. I had Smoky, Sooty, Stripey, Muckman, Tiny and Gizzy. I also had Fluffy, who was as big as a dog but who went missing on us. Stripey got killed out on the road, but we had another cat who just wandered into the garden and we called her The Second Stripey. Unfortunately, he broke his tail and had to be put to sleep.

They were all very different cats. Tiny used to eat apple and banana and he'd knock on the window to get in; he'd tap on the window with the paw. Others liked different foods like jelly food and gravy food from tins. Of the two cats I have now, they both get chicken fillets. Blacky likes lamb dried food, but Chubby gets dried food from the vet's and a bit of chicken because he's diabetic. If they don't like the food, they come up and bawl in my face.

Sooty was a real pet and she would never scratch you or do anything like that. She was very playful and would lie on her back and roll up her belly. When my grandson would come to visit, he would be talking to her and she'd be rolling up the belly and purring like mad. She was really affectionate and not a bit nasty. She used to love rambling and eventually never came back. I went searching everywhere, up and down lanes, but I never found her.

One cat that was particularly close to me was Bats. She was called that because she looked a bit like a bat, with a beautiful, small bat-like head. She was white with a bit of black and grey. She was very affectionate and such a dote. She was similar to a human and could get inside my heart. Although all the cats were special, there was something a bit different about Bats. She was a wonderful cat.

She would sit up alongside me the whole time, paw me and lie up against me in the bed. She'd tap me if she wanted anything. When I'd come back from my holidays, she would meow like mad when she saw me; she was always delighted that I was back home. She loved lying up against things; even when she'd be out in the sun, she would lie up against the railing.

When we watched the TV, Bats would sit beside me. If Sooty was there, she would be on the other side of the chair. Smoky would be over on a leather chair. That all changed when Sooty went missing and Smoky took over on the other side of the chair. Unfortunately, Bats died aged 12 and I was very upset. She probably stands out as my favourite.

You know what Gizzy used to do? Years ago, my husband and I used to walk over to the woodlands. When she'd see me putting on my coat, she'd get out the window and trail us all the way over. In the end, we'd have to get the car and bring her back. Smoky had a similar habit of following me when I went to visit my friend Mary. She'd be meowing outside of Mary's window. But a whole lot of them might follow me if I was walking up and down the garden; there could be three or four of them after me.

When I had the 28 of them, they slept outside in the shed. The place was safe. It was only when the number got down to seven that I brought them all in. They all had their own places in the house. They were all clean. They would all go to the toilet outside and then come in.

It was lovely when their little kittens were born. They were little dotes. I used to love cuddling them into me. I would even be there for the births, petting them and rubbing them. You couldn't do that with Tommy Duttons; she went under a bed and didn't want anyone around. But I was there for the two lots of Chubby's kittens. She was crying with pain and I wished I could help her. There was always something special about those events.

When I look back, the cats were all like children to me. I know they loved me and I loved every one of them with all my heart. I really took care of them and they gave me plenty of affection back. I would recommend them to anyone. They are kind-hearted, great fun and wonderful company. They are very intelligent, even though people often think they are not.

I have only the two now – Blacky, who is 17, and a new Chubby, who is 14. Blacky has to be petted the whole time, while Chubby is an old slob. The house is so lonely with so few around. But I don't think I would get any more. My heart would be broken from them. Losing them is so upsetting. That's the biggest problem with cats – it's very lonely when they die. It's like losing a member of your family, and I've had too many heartaches in my life.

**CARMELLA outlines how her beloved cat Felix refused to leave her side.**

When I was very young, over 80 years ago, I had a little black cat called Felix. He was jet-black but with a white mark, and he was very affectionate. He would rub up against me, purring and purring. I had him from when he was a kitten and he slept with me in the bed. He would meet me at the gate when I was coming home from school. I played with him all the time. I really loved him.

My sister arrived when I was eight. My mother came home with her one day. Unfortunately, every day after that, the cat would get into her pram and lie down beside her. They would take the cat out, but he would continue to go back in. My father said to me, 'We can't have this. The cat might smother your sister.' He asked me, 'Do you want your cat or do you want your sister?' I said, 'Well, I want my sister.'

He said he would take the cat down to his workplace and I could send food down to feed him. He worked across Dublin, about eight miles away from where we lived. He told me he would look after the cat for me. This he did, and he would tell me every now and again, 'Felix is doing grand.'

I was heartbroken. I really missed Felix. My parents would say, 'Well, you have a little sister to play with,' but she was just lying in her pram and not much good to me. I wasn't so fond of her, believe me. I felt, 'It's your fault that the cat went.' I then didn't hear anything about the cat for a good while. I only discovered later on that he had disappeared from my dad's workplace, but they didn't tell me that at the time.

One morning, months afterwards, we were all sitting having our breakfast when I saw a cat coming along the wall at the end of the garden. It was the most miserable specimen of a skinny cat I have ever seen. He was so thin and his sides were caved in. He jumped down into the garden and just collapsed.

I immediately recognised him. I said to my mammy, 'Felix is back!' She looked out and she realised it was him. You can't imagine my excitement. I was roaring crying. I lifted him up and cuddled him. He purred and was rubbing up against me. He was delighted to see me.

I immediately asked, 'Can I keep him? Can I keep him?' I promised I would never let him get into the pram again. My parents agreed and they promised to never let him go again. We fed him up and took him to the vet, and he was allowed to stay at home with me after that. He was back sleeping with me, down at the end of the bed.

Obviously, Felix had just walked away from where my dad worked and headed for home. How he had crossed eight miles through the city I will never know. I'm not sure how long he had been missing but it could have been anything up to six weeks or so. It's incredible to think that the cat had walked all that distance back.

Later, when I got married, my husband didn't like cats. But I loved all animals, so we always had a dog. Interestingly, after what happened, my sister had a great love of cats all her life and she always owned one. Even still, she has a cat. There must be some connection between the cat getting into her pram as a baby and her love of cats to this day.

When I look back, I think it is amazing what Felix did. It must be a sixth sense. I mean, he was brought down in the back of a car to where my father worked, so he couldn't have even seen where he was going. I am now in my mid-80s and my sister is in her late 70s and I still don't understand it. But I always think of Felix and he's still in my mind. It was so great to have him home again, back home to me.

**TOM BELL recalls a traumatic event involving a cat that occurred over a decade and a half ago.**

We bought a holiday home in Canada in the early 2000s. I had noticed a cat around the property at the time we were buying it. He was a big cat, darkish with a bit of grey. It seemed to be a family pet from the previous owner. I said to the estate agent, 'I'm a bit concerned about the cat.' I heard that the family were moving to an apartment and I was worried that they may not be allowed to keep pets there, or the cat may not settle there, or something like that.

'Don't worry,' the estate agent said. 'That's not a problem. He'll be going to some friends or relatives ten miles up the road.' I said, 'That's OK, then.' So we bought the property and returned home. It was around September and October when we were away and the weather wouldn't have been too bad.

We returned to the house around the middle of November. It was really cold. I put the thermometer outside the front door and it was minus nine in the mornings, and that wasn't even the middle of winter. The cat was there again. Where he had been in between is anybody's guess. He must have been living rough, I suppose, but the weather wouldn't have been too severe. There may have been an odd frost, but that's about it.

Suddenly, the cat started scratching at the windows to get in. He was like something possessed. You could see the marks where he scratched. He was trying to get into his old house, probably after years of coming in during the night and then heading off during the day. We were painting and doing other things, knowing that we were leaving again a few weeks later.

He was clearly looking for food, but we didn't let him in believing that to give him food would be pointless as we were going away again shortly afterwards. We were hoping he'd give up and move somewhere else. We did, however, feel misgivings and wondered what the right thing to do would be in the situation.

He scratched at the windows over a couple of days, but then he gave up. I noticed him, after that, in a field about 50 or 60 yards away. I had been walking around the property and he was sitting up on a bit of a ridge. He was looking at me with expressionless and condemning eyes. Ironically, he was sitting in a position where we could see him from the bedroom upstairs. He really didn't move from then on. Although he was alive and conscious, he must have been very weak.

I felt in the wrong, but I wondered, 'What can we do?' Even if we had brought him bread and milk, or whatever, what then would happen the next day, or the next week, when we were gone? The weather wasn't going to improve. It was about minus nine in the night and just about freezing during the day, and it was going to get worse. Even if we brought him to a neighbour, there was no guarantee he'd stay there; he might just come back to our house again.

All of a sudden, the temperature fell again by a further two or three degrees and a night came when we had some snow. I went out to look for the cat, but I couldn't see him anymore. I never saw him again. On entering the house, I felt that one creature's physical torment had ended while torment of a very different kind was about to start for another being.

What happened with that cat has lived with me ever since. Even today, in County Kerry, I still look back on it. It's one of the events you don't forget, perhaps like the birth of a first child or a first day at school. It's one of those things that stick in your mind. It's probably something I can't either write off or compensate for.

I still feel a bit of guilt over it. On the other hand, it's hard to say if that guilt is justified. The guilt maybe should belong to the previous owner or to the estate agent. I was left to pick up the pieces. It was all a mess, especially for the cat, who may have lived another ten years or more.

We kept the house in Canada for another three or four years, but the cat never turned up again. I think he's gone where we are all going to go eventually. But his scratch marks lived on; they remained on the windows in the house, and I can still see them in my mind today.

# UNCONVENTIONAL
# FRIENDS

Winston Churchill kept most unusual pets. The former British Prime Minister owned pigs, bantams, swans, goldfish and butterflies. He also acquired a leopard named Sheba, a lion named Rota and kangaroos as gifts over the years.

His pets were often strangely named. There was Dodo, his bulldog, followed by other dogs named Peas, Pink Poo and Rufus, and a cute marmalade cat called Jock. Only when Jock arrived at the table could meals be served.

He had another cat, called Mickey. One day, while he was talking to the Lord Chancellor on the telephone, Mickey was playing with the cable. 'Get off the line, you fool!' he shouted, before apologising profusely to the astonished man.

Following his death, at his family's request, a marmalade cat named Jock has always roamed Chartwell, his former estate. As the following stories reveal, the eclectic spirit of Churchill lives on to this day.

ANTOINETTE **had a gander named Lucifer, who was as close to her as any pet could ever be.**

We used to live in the countryside in County Wicklow. We lived in a really old Tudor-style house, with a lot of forestry around us. It was beautiful but we were plagued with robberies, lots of them. My husband came up with this idea that we would get geese for protection and to stop break-ins. If they attack you, they can cause incredible damage. I said, 'I don't know about that!'

As it happened, a friend of mine said, 'A friend of ours has got geese and they're going to be eaten for Christmas. There are six of them. Do you want them?' When I heard that, I felt myself going all funny. I said, 'Bring them up to me. I won't be eating them but I'll keep them for protection.' When they arrived, they were only chicks. So I ended up with six of them and they got bigger and bigger until they were like swans.

Although we got them for protection, they eventually became pets. The biggest pet of them all was the male gander fellow who came, too. At first, we thought that he was female so I called him Lucy, but then I christened him Lucifer because we discovered he was male and also because of the damage he eventually caused. He ended up living with all his females on a water area and island that we built for them. It was an area of about half an acre that we dug out and put water into. They started breeding there and I eventually ended up with 19 of them.

Lucifer was very possessive of me and attached to me, so he would guard the place and protect me. He was very powerful and vicious. For example, when cars would drive in, Lucifer would go around the cars and let no one out of them. One visitor had to actually drive away because she couldn't get out of her car. This was before mobile phones so she had to go elsewhere and ring me. When my husband came home, he would have to take his coat off and, just like a bullfighter, try to get past Lucifer and into the house.

Lucifer was a wonderful character. He would answer to his name. Although he was named Lucifer, I would call him Lucy Lou when people were there because I thought that his name was dreadful. He had a very powerful personality and he really had the rest of the geese under control. Wherever he'd walk, the others would walk behind him. He'd also be delighted when he'd see me come home. When I'd stop the car at the gate, he'd be running around all excited.

Lucifer would come into the kitchen and jump up on the couch near the lovely log fire. I would then feed him bread. He loved that as a treat. He also loved scones with the sultanas in them. He'd actually sit there with the legs crossed, as if he was out of a cartoon. My husband would say, 'This is crazy! You have that yoke in the kitchen and I can't get in!' He was a real character, unbelievable.

The other geese wouldn't come in because Lucifer wouldn't let them. He'd stop them at the door and wouldn't allow them inside. He was very territorial like that. He also followed me around. No matter where I went, he was after me. Then, once he'd hear a car coming up the road, he'd run with his neck down and he'd be hissing at the gate and no one would get in. Needless to say, we had no break-ins after he arrived.

We had two dogs at the time and one of them decided to chase Lucifer. I think the dog got jealous because I was petting him. Lucifer liked to be stroked under the chin. The dog got him by the neck and tried to drown him in the water area. It was about 15 feet deep. I had an awful job getting the dog away. I also worried that foxes might get them, but they didn't. They had killed some ducks we used to own. But I think the foxes were too smart to tackle Lucifer or the rest of them.

Eventually, we decided to sell the house and I didn't want to leave the geese behind because I was so worried about them. There were people down in Leitrim who had lakes and they said, 'You can bring them down and let them out into the wild.' I was initially afraid that they wouldn't survive. But we decided to go ahead with the plan.

We got this trailer and we put the whole lot of them into it and headed off to Leitrim. It was gas. Every time we went under a bridge, they'd put their heads down. It was very funny. Lucifer was going mad; he knew there was a move going on and he was very worried about it. I felt guilty because they had nearly become domesticated.

Eventually, we put them all into the lake, including Lucifer. He just looked back and then took off. I was in bits. I asked myself, 'Are they going to survive? What will happen to them?' The owners of the place knew I was worried and they said, 'Don't ever come back, because he will not forget you. Once you'd call, he'd hear you. It would be cruel to come back.'

However, about a year later, I did go back. I looked over to one of the lakes and there they were on the island. They had multiplied and there were even more of them there, no doubt including Lucifer. I suppose he was lucky he didn't end up in a duvet or on the Christmas table! Instead, he and all his pals are flying wild around Leitrim and having a great time. If you ever go down there, you'd want to watch out because Lucifer is probably patrolling the area!

**JOSEPHINE CURRAN and her sister developed a close bond with a wild mouse over half a century ago. She still remembers the mouse to this day.**

When I was about 11 and my sister was about 14, we would do our homework in the kitchen of our family house. It would be about seven or eight in the evening. The radio would have been turned off and we were both supposed to sit down and concentrate. We would be there for about an hour or an hour and a half, depending on what we had to do.

We would sit at a table under the window in the kitchen. My father would be reading in the sitting-room and my mother used to work at night. My granny supervised, but she would be elsewhere in the house and only came to tell us it was time to go to bed. Everything was very, very quiet.

One particular night, we heard a little crinkle near the press where my mother kept the saucepans. We looked over and we saw a little head peeping around a corner. It was a tiny little mouse. He was grey and only about two inches long, with little ears and a long tail. I said, 'Isn't he cute-looking?' We both thought he was lovely.

We decided we'd get something for him, so we got a bit of cheese from the other end of the kitchen and he came out to eat it. We thought he'd smell the cheese and like it. We watched him eating and he disappeared quickly after that. We went to bed without mentioning a word about what had happened. We certainly didn't mention it to our granny.

The following night, we looked over and there he was again. He was peeping around as if to say, 'I'm back!' We decided that we would have to give him something once again, which we did. After a week or so, we were still giving him food – cheese and bread and a little bit of meat. He'd eat it all, although not very quickly because he was small. We also chose a name for him – we called him Timmy.

This went on for a couple of weeks. He was getting closer and closer, and he would nearly take the food off our hand at this stage. He appeared every school night. At weekends, we would put a few crumbs behind the press so he wouldn't be hungry. We were praying he wouldn't appear at weekends because we didn't want them to know he was there. We knew if he did come out what the end result would be.

We both grew to like him and enjoy his visits. He was a bit of entertainment. We were watching him and wondering what he was going to do. He used always keep a lookout. His eyes were darting all over the place. He was obviously aware of the danger that he was in. If he had come from outside, which he probably did, everything was strange to him anyway.

I suppose, in those days, we were more easily entertained. We had no television. We didn't get a television set until I was in secondary school. Even though the radio would have been on all evening, it wasn't on when we were doing our homework. So the mouse was a big attraction to the two of us. He was something new.

One night, we were feeding the mouse when suddenly we heard something from behind us. It was our granny. She hadn't announced herself. She must have thought things were too quiet, so she decided to check. She had a habit of appearing quietly. I can still picture her, with the long nightdress and the hair brushed out. She was just standing there, watching us feeding the mouse.

'I'll sort him,' she said. 'Oh, no, you can't do that!' we replied. We were upset over it, but she didn't say any more; she just left. We knew her attitude to mice was that they were things to be got rid of, but we thought, 'She's not going to do anything about it.' We were horrified and hoped the mouse would escape. I even left the door open that night and the next day in the hope he'd go out.

The next evening, we were sitting at the table, doing our homework, when we heard a loud bang. We hadn't realised that our granny had actually put down a trap. It was around the corner of the press, but we couldn't see it from where we were sitting. I was facing the press and my sister was sideways to it.

We got up and saw the trap. The mouse was dead. If he had just been caught in the trap, we could have left him off. Instead, he was stone dead. The trap had come down over his head; he didn't stand a chance. Our granny heard the sound and came in and said, 'Got it!' We were devastated, really sick. We didn't like our granny for a good while after that, but she was a lovely woman and we eventually forgave her.

I suppose times were very different back then. People weren't sentimental about animals. If my granny wanted fresh chicken, she could go out and twist the neck of a chicken and put it on to cook. If you needed food, you just killed something, and that was it. Equally, mice were vermin and had to be killed. Doing it was no big deal.

My sister and I often talked about the mouse after that. He'd come up in conversation years later. One of us would say, 'Do you remember the little mouse?' It still goes on to this day. We wouldn't necessarily be emotional about it, but we would think back fondly on him and what happened all those years ago. Not a lot of things stick in your mind but Timmy did, especially after the trauma of him being killed.

We had other animals to interest us after that. My father bred young Greyhounds and we always had a dog who we loved. But the mouse was something else. We had him for weeks and we had enjoyed him immensely. We really fancied him as a pet, but our friendship only got so far. We had formed a nice little bond with him, and then he was gone.

**ANN O'BRIEN explains how two cygnets became long-term guests at her family's farm.**

It was a neighbour who first saw the two cygnets. They were sitting on their own. There's a stream close to us which comes down through a glen and woods and out into the ocean, and she saw them on rocks at the end of that stream. She said it to my father, Patrick Allen, and he went the following day to have a look.

He drove there with my mother and my aunt. He saw them there and knew they weren't going to survive. They were very young and a fawn-grey colour. He brought the two of them home in the boot at the front of his Volkswagen.

There's a funny side to what happened. My aunt was very religious and my father said he never heard so many swears or curses out of her because the cygnets got so excited when they got into the car, and you can imagine what they did! She was probably blessing herself and cursing at the same time!

The two cygnets were brought back to the house. My father then dug a hole in the garden and he put plastic, water and muddy clay into it. The two cygnets went into it straightaway. There was a dog kennel nearby and they would sleep in it. They settled in and were very happy.

One was male, the other female, and my father called them Dan and Sal. They were just two names chosen at random. I'd say the minute he saw them, that's what he called them. It's like Bonnie and Clyde. They were simple names; they came straight into his head, and that was it.

We had a farm and they would go up to the yard, where the calves were, and they'd eat the calves' food. They'd eat greens or scraps, everything. Beyond that, they kept to themselves a lot. To me, it looked like a boring life, mainly because you would think swans would have exciting things going on, but they didn't.

They did go for walks with my father. I think they took to him more than to either my twin sister or me. We were about 13 or 14 at the time. If given a choice to walk after us or my father, they would choose him. They would follow him wherever he went.

They'd follow him up and down the drills when he'd be ploughing. They'd be with him when he'd be cleaning out calf houses or giving water to the horse. If they heard him or his car coming back, they'd go over to him. They'd be around everywhere, especially when my father would be there.

I often asked my father how come they weren't killed on the road. He explained that the roads weren't busy then. Even if they were busy, it wouldn't have mattered because they would never go out on the road on their own. Nor did they ever make any effort to head for the tide, which is only a few hundred yards away.

Their appearance changed a lot over time. When they arrived first, they were fawn-grey and you wouldn't give them a second look. Eventually, though, they turned out to be elegant and very beautiful, just as swans are. The male swan became much whiter than the female. We wondered about that because they must have been the same age when they were found. Maybe they were from different nests, who knows? Either way, they were beautiful.

After about a year, my father knew they were getting ready to leave. They took off, one day, on a little walk of their own. They went up to the top of the field. It was just the two of them; my father wasn't with them. Then they came back again.

They also started looking up in the air. Then, for a good few weeks, they started taking off and coming back. It was clear they needed to go, although they wanted to stay. One day, they circled around the house and left.

For three or four years after that, they came back every year. They'd fly over the house. It would make you shiver thinking of it. The hair would stand up on the back of your neck as you'd watch them. It was like they were thankful. Sometimes, my father would hope that they'd land, but they never did.

Even today, many, many years later, I look at different places where I see swans and wonder if they are there or if their offspring are there. If I saw two swans now coming over the house, nobody could stop me from being convinced it was them. We have lovely memories of them and my father still gets sad about them. He sometimes even has a tear in his eye when we remember them. But we had them for a year, and they had to go.

**SHEILA KENNEDY tells of a dog that adopted her in a most unconventional way and decided to come to stay.**

I used to go for a walk every day with my dog Mitzi. She was a fairly young Springer Spaniel. I would go down a hill, over to the beach, across the beach, and then back up again. It was a good mile of a walk. We used to pass another house on the way, which had dogs.

One particular dog used to bark at the two of us as we would pass by. She was like a sheepdog or a 'cattle dog', I suppose. She was about ten years old at the time. She'd be running up and down the wall outside the house, barking at us. I didn't like it and I didn't really like her very much, as a result.

My dog was about eight years old at that stage. She was a beautiful dog. All she wanted to do was play with a ball. She loved going on her walks because she'd get a ball thrown to her all the time. If you stopped to talk to people, she would keep barking until you started moving again. She really was a lovely dog.

Eventually, she started getting fits and we couldn't control them. She was unwell and had to be put to sleep. After she was gone, I continued to go for walks on my own, but I noticed the barking from the other dog had stopped. Once Mitzi wasn't there, the dog never barked. Instead, she would start wagging her tail and coming out to meet me.

Within a week, that dog – who I discovered was called Jess – started following me back up the road. The first day, she came just a little bit up the road. The next day, she came a bit further. Then she started coming to the house. She did it bit by bit.

Eventually, she started coming into the house and taking over. She was delighted with herself. Within a couple of weeks, she had decided to stay. She was totally different from the dog I had met before. She started following me everywhere and became like my shadow. She turned out to be the grandest dog ever, absolutely gorgeous, very affectionate.

She would join me on walks. When she did, she would not pass the house she came from. She would go through a gate, down through a big field and out through another gate, where she'd wait for me until I had passed the house. She would do the same thing on the way back.

I tried to bring her home loads of times. I might walk her down the hill and let her continue while I ran the other way, but it didn't work. Sometimes, I'd put her in the car and drive her down. I'd then drive away as fast as I could so she wouldn't follow me. But she'd be back up at the house ahead of me.

As it happened, the man who owned her was a lovely man and had loads of dogs. He was very good with them. He would train them really well. If a car came, she would stand in. If you were on the beach and you told her to sit and wait, she would obey you. He had looked after her and trained her well. He was very good about what had happened and he used to be asking me about her.

Somehow, she had taken a liking to me. Perhaps it was that all of a sudden there was no competition from my previous dog. Maybe she saw that I had lost my companion. On the other hand, I reckon there were so many dogs where she had been that she was delighted with all the attention being focused directly on her. She probably liked the bit of peace, as well.

She was an oldish dog when she came to stay. Unlike Mitzi, there was no play in her. Instead, she was a very wise dog. She would look up at me very knowledgeably. She would also be watching me. I felt she was guarding me all the time. Wherever I'd go, she would be two steps behind me.

She also protected the house. One day, when I came home, I discovered that the house had been broken into. It was clear the people who broke in had dropped everything. She probably had been stretched out on the settee in the front room. They came in the kitchen window and I'd say she attacked them. She clearly put the run on them. She certainly saved my bacon that day.

She was here for about five or six years. Eventually, her back legs went. When she'd come to the beach, she'd sit down at the beginning of it, let me have my walk, and then she'd join me on the way back home again. She got so bad that they could do nothing with her. She couldn't stand up and was dragging herself around. I couldn't put her through that, so I had to put her to sleep.

Her death broke my heart. I had become very attached to her. She had gone everywhere with me and she really had been a gentle old soul. She was a really lovely dog, very intelligent and, above all, she chose me. I think the fact that she chose me made her special. It made her stand out above all the dogs I've ever known.

**JODIE loved the pigs her grandfather kept on his farm back in the 1950s.**

My grandfather was a farmer and he kept pigs. I loved them. They were kept in the pig house beside the family home. There was always great warmth in there. I would go to see them from the time I was a toddler, about three years of age. I would later go up there practically every day of the week.

I probably had names for the pigs, but at this stage I can't remember what they were. What I do remember is their colour, which I loved; it might be why pink is my favourite colour to this day! I especially liked the baby ones and the little squealy noises they made.

I loved watching them eat. When my grandfather would be feeding them, he'd say, 'Don't come in. You wait there.' He'd say that because the sows can be quite vicious. But I'd go in and watch.

The minute he arrived at the door with the pot, they'd be waiting. They'd be squealing and all excited. They'd be falling over and trying to get to the food. As a child, you'd be laughing at them stumbling over each other and struggling to get something to eat.

Every day, especially in the cold weather, they'd get a warm meal. He'd serve it out to them. They wouldn't stop eating until the dishes would be clean. They'd gobble it all up. I'd love the snorting noises they'd make when they were snuffling around and eating.

I would go with him in late autumn to collect leaves and make bedding for them. He'd give us a bag to fill. You'd think you'd have it full but he'd put his foot in, push the leaves right down to the bottom and say, 'There you go. Fill it up.' Eventually, when the pigs would be finished with them, the leaves would go on the compost heap.

I'd hate it when the pigs would be taken away and sold. It was like killing someone in the family. How can you put a name on an animal and then put it on the table for dinner? I had murder with my father over that issue. We had a lot of hens and every so often my Uncle Paddy would come and kill one. I didn't know that the chicken on the table had been outside, running around.

One day, Daddy decided he'd have a go at it. He'd never done it before. He had the hen's legs tied and he was trying to kill it. I was really upset. I kept telling Daddy he was a murderer. The others were all laughing at me. It took me a while, until I was about ten or 11, to realise that the same thing happened with pigs; the rashers and bacon were the pigs that I had been picking nuts for and throwing bits of food to not long before.

The only days I didn't go to visit my grandfather were the days he was going to sell the pigs. After he sold them, he'd come home on the bus and call in to see Mammy and the rest of us. He'd always bring an Oxford Lunch from Johnston, Mooney and O'Brien's, a Toblerone and Yorkshire Toffees. He'd have a slice of cake and then he'd walk on home and continue his day's work. They were memorable days for us.

Looking back, I think pigs have unfairly got a bad reputation. Some people call them dirty. Maybe it was because I was brought up with them since I was tiny, but I really loved them. They were almost pets to me. As a child, I mightn't have thought that, but that's what they were.

I look back very fondly on them now. They were part of my childhood and part and parcel of my life at the time. I suppose most kids today would look back on their first computer game, or something like that, but not me. I look back on going in and seeing the pigs. They bring back lovely memories.

**Mick O'Connell has had a lifelong attachment to ferrets, the finest creatures he has ever seen.**

The first one I got was from Northern Ireland. I bought it in the 1950s, when I was going to school. It was around 1957 or 1958. I saw an ad and I sent away for it. It arrived down to County Cork by bus. It was in a cardboard box with holes in it. I think it was a Wednesday and I was all excited. The bus conductor, as he was handing me the box, said, 'I think this is something in the style of a ferret! It's better for you to handle it than me!'

The ferret was a doe and she was beautiful. She was a polecat and was black-coloured. At the time I got her, she was about five inches long, just a little baby. I knew what to expect because my father had kept them before. He had died when I was only around eight and the ferrets had passed on, too. I wanted to get back into keeping them for myself.

I called her Tippy and I had a cage made up for her, which contained a little bed. Outside that cage was another cage with sawdust. I fed her mince and milk with bread. I then trained her to get used to the dogs I had at the time. Very soon, she wouldn't take a bit of notice of the dogs and they wouldn't take a bit of notice of her.

It was amazing to see how well she got on with the dogs. She'd start to hum, which is how ferrets communicate. She'd be bucking around and the dogs would be running around the place. They'd love it. One dog used to catch her in her mouth, just like a lion catching a pup, and then she'd let her go. They had great fun together.

I eventually got more ferrets. I ended up with about five at a maximum. I bought them in places like Waterford and Tipperary. I got one albino, who was snow-white. I also bought some liners, who are dark but very big. I even had one as big as an otter. I might be in the kitchen and there could be three or four of them sitting around.

I remember, at one stage, there were five sisters of mine living in our house. I'd put the ferrets into the bed with them. Even though they were used to them from my father, my sisters would give a nice bit of a scream. They'd boot the ferrets out quickly. They'd boot me out, too!

I brought one to school in a box. I took it in with me to a nun. I opened up the box and I was sure she was going to jump, but she didn't. I was surprised to discover that she had a farming background and understood about wildlife. She knew all about ferrets and appreciated them. She was actually delighted.

The other kids loved them, too. They could put their hands on them and hold them and do what they liked with them. They would see me with them and they knew I had the ferrets well-trained. They gave me a nickname because of my love of nature. They called me Thorn.

I was known around town for my gift as a trainer. I had some sort of touch with the ferrets. I would train the dogs, too. I had one particular dog, Sandy, who was a cross between a terrier and a Cocker Spaniel. Whatever I would ask her to fetch, she would bring it back. I would ask her to get a ferret. The dog would go down the stairs, through the hall and out the back. The cage was up a small bit and she'd reach up and open a latch.

It often happened that I'd arrive home from work and the ferrets would be out of their cages. The dog would be after leaving them out. They would be inside in the bed with the dog. She obviously wanted a bit of company. When they'd hear me coming, they would be all excited. 'Mick is going to feed us!' they'd be thinking, so they would all run into my flat.

I trained them to go hunting, but not for killing. I'd bring the ferrets and the dogs, and we'd hunt. I would go off down the fields. On weekends, when there would be no school, I'd leave at six o'clock in the morning and be out until six o'clock at night. I did it every Saturday and Sunday. That was my life.

I wouldn't care if they got nothing in a day. I just loved seeing them working. I also loved the day out, the wildlife, and I loved going to places with scenery. I'd love seeing the country. I'd see badgers and otters and all types of ducks and swans. I'd go into woodlands. I'd be there in deep snow and I'd see deer. I'd just sit down and admire what I was seeing, but I was never a man for killing.

I have a nephew who called to me one day after hunting. He was sitting on the settee. 'Uncle Michael, were you out today?' he asked. 'I was,' I replied. 'It was a grand day for it,' he said. He didn't know it but the ferrets were in behind the settee, asleep after the day.

He pushed back on the settee and they all came running out under his legs. Whatever movement he made woke them up. He actually jumped. There was a table in front of him; he hit it. He drove both the table and me into the fire with the fright that he got. He got the shock of his life.

I stopped keeping ferrets about five years ago. I gave them up because I had been born with a chest weakness and it started getting worse and worse. I had to attend doctors and I'm now on medication, so I can't travel long distances without getting out of breath. I had to rest, so I gave up the ferrets although I kept a few dogs.

They were beautiful to keep. They would lie in front of the fire, along with the dogs. They'd sit up on the sofa alongside of me; the dogs would be there, too. There was no jealousy in them. They were just as affectionate as a dog and they would know you as well.

I'd recommend them to anybody. Since I was going to school, I always loved wildlife. I have loved all kinds of animals, but I especially loved ferrets. They are wonderful company, lovely creatures and beautiful pets. I'm 71 now, and if I had my life to live over I'd have three, four or even five of them again, no hesitation. They really are unique.

**BERNARD BURKE believes there's nothing to beat donkeys for love and affection.**

I have five donkeys and my grandnieces have given names to them. They call one Cheryl Cole, another is Simon Cowell, a third is Louis Walsh and a fourth is Gary Barlow. I think they must have been watching *The X Factor*! They have no name on the baby one yet, although I think they are considering Pixie. I don't know where that name came from.

I have different names for three of them. I call the three – a male, a female and a foal – Jesus, Mary and Joseph, because they look to me like the Holy Family of Nazareth when they go around together. The daddy is pure black; the mother is brown with a dark line across her back and also across both shoulders, like a sign of the cross. They are cheerful and friendly, just like the other donkeys.

A lot of people think they are not clever. They might say, 'Oh! He's an ass!' when they refer to someone, implying that he is as thick as a donkey. But they are not thick; they are extremely intelligent. For example, they can open gates. There are gates with L-shaped levers that pull back. They can pull them back with their mouths. They then head off to somewhere interesting.

About two years ago, in summer, I was having a bite to eat in the back kitchen and the door was open. The next thing, they appeared at the door. As it happened, I had a few apples and they were happy with them. I then put them back in their field.

Another time, they turned up in a nearby house just to see what the neighbours were like. They stood at the door. They were being nosy. The man came out with his young boy, who was delighted to see them. The neighbours were happy and it seems the donkeys were pleased to have checked them out.

On a further occasion, when they went visiting a different neighbour, they discovered a lovely miniature apple tree. The neighbour had the apple tree in a tub at the front of the house. She was in town, but when she came home there were no apples left. They must have spotted the apples at some time when they were passing by. By the time she came home, they had left. They left no sign that they were there, but the gate was open!

They are very affectionate. When I go out in the morning, they are waiting for me. The first thing I do is give all five a hug. They love that. Sometimes, when I'm not coming in a hurry, they will start braying. They want me out. When they see me, they are happy.

I mostly feed them oats and some hay, but they also love chocolate and crisps. There's nothing they like more than for you to pour out the crisps on your hand. They will gently take them; they won't bite you. They love a piece of chocolate and they'll chew on it. But they also love apples and carrots.

They often lie down together in the field. They will stay in a group. The mother will lie down with her foal right next to her. The others will then lie in a circle around them. They are protecting the mother and the foal. They don't mind if I come along; they are always happy to see me. But if another animal came along, or someone wandered into the field, they would be protective.

For the wintertime, I have a shed I put them into. They can lie down in the shed and they get plenty to eat. The winter can be hard on them, but they have plenty of warmth and shelter in the shed. There is something biblical about them. When

Jesus was born, wasn't there a donkey in the stable? And didn't Jesus ride a donkey into Jerusalem? As someone said, 'Wasn't the donkey the Lord's Rolls-Royce?'

When the donkeys have foals, they always seem to deliver them at night. When you go out in the morning, the foal is there. I also remember, one night, I came home late and I went to have a look at the animals. It was a moonlit night, about half past one in the morning. I went to a certain spot in the field and I thought I heard funny noises.

At that time, I had two donkeys and one was ill. Unfortunately, it had died in the field. The other donkey was there, standing over it, crying. He never stopped. I had to get the dead donkey taken away to have it buried. But the other donkey – the friend – couldn't stop crying.

I saw the same thing another time when I was coming home one night. Two donkeys had been on the road – a mother and son – and the little baby donkey had been hit by a car and killed. The mother was there, standing over it and not braying but crying. It was so sad.

The only thing donkeys can't do is talk to you, although they have their own ways of communicating. They brush alongside you. When you hug them, they press against you. They press tightly as if they are saying, 'Oh! Thank you!' for whatever it is you have done. You can also tell what they are feeling by the look in their eyes.

They are really beautiful animals, God's creatures. There is nothing to match a donkey for affection or love. I'm afraid that phrase 'as thick as an ass' doesn't wash with me. They're far from it. They are very intelligent and lovely to have around. They must be the most beautiful animals of all.

**Ann O'Brien tells the story of how a wild fox lived with her family in the 1960s.**

One day, our family dog Lassie brought a tiny fox cub back home. He was blue-grey in colour. She used to go into a nearby farm and must have come across him there. He was uninjured and didn't seem to have been left too long on his own. Maybe he had been abandoned or got lost, who knows?

My father, Patrick Allen, thinks that the fox might have been about nine or ten weeks old. He still had that fluffy, furry coat. What do you do with a cub like that? Land him back out in a field again? My father christened him Timothy and decided to keep him.

There was an old chicken coop outside and he slept in that. He was treated well. He ate whatever was going, like bread and milk. He became a great friend of Lassie and felt that she was taking care of him. And she was. That's the kind of character Lassie was – she was a gentle old soul.

At the beginning, my father wore very thick gloves when he was dealing with Timothy. He knew animals very well and he also understood that foxes are not to be tamed. Eventually, however, the fox started to trust my father and they would go for walks together.

Lassie loved him. They were great friends and they'd play with each other all the time. They would tumble around on the grass like any two dogs would do. Lassie would also go into his house with him. They really got on together. If anything, Lassie might be a bit jealous if you went near him.

Timothy would also come into our house on a daily basis. When my mother would light the fire, he'd come in. He loved it in front of the fire. My father always had a long lead on him just in case anyone came to the door. It became so normal for us to have him in the house that you'd forget he was there.

When my sister Mary and I would be going off to bed at nine o'clock, he'd bark and scratch at the door to get into our room; he really wanted to get down to us. We also wore big bows in our hair. If Mary knelt down, he would get up on her knee, sit on her lap and take the slides or the ribbon off her hair. He never did that with me; maybe I wasn't as brave at the time.

There wasn't magic every day. Although he was friendly, you wouldn't want to be bringing him to where there would be too many people. You might be going to the beach and he'd want to come with you, but we couldn't take him. Even though he was friendly with us, and especially with my father, we didn't leave him near children.

As Timothy headed into his second year with us, my father realised that he wasn't going to stay. He used to go away for a few hours and come back. He started staying away longer and longer. One evening, it was dark and he wasn't back. We had turkeys, at that stage, and they started to disappear. For a while, he would still come back for the night, but then he just went and was gone.

It was sad when he left and I'd imagine he didn't have a very good ending. He was domesticated, quite tame, so he would have found it hard to survive. We never saw him again, but he is long remembered and regularly spoken about and we have photographs of him to remind us of what he was like.

It was great for me and my sister to have him when we were growing up. We really loved him. We always liked animals, but Timothy was a novelty and we knew we had to take care of him. That's what we did. He was really nice to have around, especially when we were only about ten or 11 years old, or so, at the time.

We never mollycoddled him or put bows on him or anything like that. He wasn't just a showpiece. He was an animal and we always felt that he might want to leave us and go back to the wild. For about two years, though, he was part of the family, and he was a beautiful animal to have around.

**JEREMIAH talks about the beauty and calm nature of his two pet goats.**

We decided to get some goats a few years ago. I always heard they were calm, beautiful creatures. A lot of farmers, long ago, used to bring a goat into the herd, believing there would be no diseases or that the cows wouldn't drop calves. We had a bit of ground and it was wasted, so I made a phone call and set up a meeting to acquire some goats.

My son and I headed off, one day, and we ended up in a field where goats appeared out of hedges and ditches. It was in the middle of nowhere. My son suddenly pointed at one and said, 'We'll have that one!' We ended up getting two of them.

The first night that we got them home, they escaped and took off. We had to follow them in two cars and go around looking for them. They went across main roads and jumped ditches. We had to chase them everywhere. We finally had to get ropes and walk them home.

We thought they might have been going back home, but it's more likely they sensed other goats nearby. Females have this extraordinary sense of smell which they use to detect male goats. If they are in heat, they can break out and travel the country. It's more likely that's why they escaped.

One of the goats really took to my son, and my son took to her. The goat would look for him in the house. She would run from a distance, at speed, and land on the windowsill with her four legs. She would then turn her head and look in the window at him. If she couldn't find him in one room, she'd go to another window and look in to see if she could see him there.

She would be calling to him. When he'd go out, he'd sit on a bucket in front of her. She'd be licking his face and rubbing his shoulders and scratching herself off him. The relationship was unreal. No matter what he did, she'd hop to it.

Goats really are wonderful creatures. They are easy to feed. We give them rolled barley and nuts. They also eat hay, but they'd eat anything. If you brought them into a field which was full of briars and ivy, they'd eat it all. They'd eat the trees and the bark off trees. They'd demolish your most beautiful shrubs. I'm hardly joking when I say that they'd eat yourself!

They also love heights. If you have a bit of ground containing only four square feet of raised land, a goat would perch on top of it. If one goat is on the raised land, the other will circle around and knock it off with her horns. The one that's been knocked off will come back, circle around and blow the other one off. They really love high ground. If there is any mound of earth there, they want to be on it.

They are very loyal and protective. I remember, at one time, two dogs came into where we keep them. I was there at the time. The dogs were fairly substantial in size and they were barking. At this stage, one of the goats had damaged one of her legs so she had only three legs to work off.

The dogs were edging towards me. Didn't she surround me and walk around my legs, protecting me! She then made a full headlock straight for the two dogs. They both disappeared off outside the fence and continued to bark outside. To protect me, she came back over and she surrounded me once again. The dogs eventually went away.

That same goat likes to get her damaged leg massaged. If I am sitting near her, perhaps on a stool with my leg half-bent before me, she will stretch out her leg onto my lap. I will then give her physio. I might be feeding her and her head would be in the bucket, but she'd stick up her leg for me to massage.

She'd lick my ear and my face, and she might have a nibble off my hair just to let me know she is grateful. She'd also lick my hands. That might be partly because of the salt on human skin. It might also be pure affection. I prefer to think it is the latter.

She would also scratch her neck off your back and put her chin on your shoulder. While one of them does that, the other has always been a bit standoffish. But that one is now coming around and is doing it, as well. She will give me a lick now, although it's not quite like the other one who would lick you to death.

I am delighted that we got them, and my son still loves them. There really is a healing in them. There's a calming influence about them, and a great sense of peace. I would now go out and spend an hour talking to them; they're like that. You'd be stone mad about them. If you want affection being returned to you, there's nothing better than a goat.

JOHN AND SHEILA KENNEDY **had unusual pets – two cows named Bingbell and Shirley.**

Sheila said she would like an animal, so I bought her a cow. I picked out a particular one because I liked the shape of her. She was an ordinary black-and-white Friesian. I knew nothing about her technically, but I thought she had a nice flat back. We christened her Bluebell, but our son couldn't pronounce the name when he was small so he used to call her Bingbell. We had great fun with her.

Bingbell eventually had a calf and our daughter Alice wanted to keep it. She was a Charolais cross, fawn with a white head, and we called her Shirley. She ended up being the greatest pet ever. We still have a picture of her on our sideboard. They were with us for decades and just about drew the old age pension with us.

At the beginning, we were real greenhorns, total novices. We hardly knew one end of a cow from another. I knew a bit from when I was a child because my father had a cow or two. Sheila had never milked a cow in her life, but she managed. We also would have been no good as farmers because we became too fond of animals and couldn't let them go.

We were lucky, though, because we had enough land to keep them. We also had a man down the hill from us who was very good about animals. If we were in trouble, we'd go to him and ask him to come up. He'd arrive and advise us. He was really great. Nine times out of ten there would be nothing wrong; on most of the other times he'd know what to do. If he couldn't help us, we'd get the vet.

After a while, we became close to Bingbell and Shirley and we grew really fond of them. In particular, our daughter Alice loved Shirley. She could go up to her, rub her and walk around her, and Shirley would never touch her. For other people, there was always the danger that you might get a puck or be chased out of the field, but she never did that with our Alice.

They also got to know us. They would arrive down to the fence when they'd notice us. For farmers with ordinary cattle in their fields, they wouldn't do that. They also became very, very clever. If we were cutting the grass outside, they would know immediately there would be a bit of grass out of the lawnmower. They'd come running down to the gate to get the little bit of grass to eat.

We could have let them go dry, but we never did. We had to get them in calf every year so they'd produce milk. We made up a milking machine and a little dairy of our own. We bought a separator, with two spouts – one for cream, the other for skim milk. We were able to make butter, as well.

While it was interesting making the cheese and the yogurt and things like that, it was a lot of hard work, too, and it tied you down. Every time you came home, you had to milk the cows. It could be any hour of the night. You would be up there with a torch, sitting under a cow, and you could be anywhere.

As they'd get to know you, they'd become brave and they might chase you. If you had a dog, they'd go to chase the dog but he'd go behind you so they'd chase you instead. You'd be in trouble then. They could also be cross. If you went near their calf, they wouldn't be too happy about it. If they thought they'd get away with it, they'd knock the bucket over when you'd be milking them. They'd kick it over.

There were plenty of dramatic events through the years. On one occasion, Shirley was looking for a mate for herself and she took off from our house. She just disappeared. We knew that if she met a car she would have just kept going and the outcome would have been awful. We had the neighbours out looking for her. We eventually found her about five miles away and brought her home.

On another night, it wasn't the two cows but three of their bullocks which created a stir. It was snowing. Our shed wasn't the best, so we headed up in the snow with hammers and nails and boards. We got them into the shed and nailed everything closed so they would be nice and cosy. We were just down by the house when we heard a bang. The whole side was out of the shed. The three bullocks were coming behind us. They were left outside that night, we're sorry to say!

They really became an important part of our lives and we worried about them. They could sense things about you. They were intelligent, too. We grew attached to them, even though most of the people where we lived must have thought we were mad. They are probably still laughing at us.

Unfortunately, we had to have Bingbell put down when she was 18. Her legs had gone. We nearly killed ourselves attempting to roll her over in the shed, trying to get her up again, but we didn't succeed. We buried her in a field. That wasn't so bad because at least she was buried nearby.

Shirley was there for some years afterwards, but eventually she got sick and we had to have her put down, too. We had to get the vet out to give her an injection. We had to get a man to come along with a lorry and take her away. We wanted to bury her on our own land, especially on account of her being our daughter's pet, but regulations would no longer allow that. It was really sad. We hated that.

Keeping the cows as pets was an interesting experiment, but it was hard work. The worst part was when they became old. It's grand when they are young and everything is going well, but when they become old and decrepit it's not so good. We were far too sentimental. That's the problem – if you're not a farmer, you're in trouble. Because of that, we probably wouldn't do it again. I think we'd stick to the dogs and the cats!

**BERNARD BURKE also loves cows and he has seven of them. He keeps them more as pets than for their commercial value.**

I have kept cows for years. I have seven now and they are all black. They are an Aberdeen Angus breed and they are easy to manage in the West of Ireland climate. I used to keep them part-time while I worked elsewhere, but now that I am retired they are more like pets or a hobby than anything else.

I open up the window early in the morning and this lowing competition starts. They are standing there at the gate waiting for the window to open up. The way they communicate is by lowing or mooing. It's as if they are saying, 'We're waiting for you! Where are you?' It's very funny.

They only quieten down when I go to them. I then put them into a different field for the day. When I walk ahead, they will follow in a line after me. I don't have a dog and I don't need one. My brother-in-law said to me one day, 'If anybody sees you, you'll be fodder for the men with the white coats!'

They are really very affectionate. If I'm in the shed with them, walking among them, they might rub up against me. They also love it when I give them a rub on their backs. They don't move when I do it. They really like the attention and they radiate an awful lot of love. They are definitely full of affection.

You can see that especially when a calf is born. The calf is lying there and you make sure the mouth is clear and the ears are cleaned out. Then the cow comes along and licks the calf. The love she shows for it is immense. Within half an hour, the calf is standing up and getting the cow's milk. The bond between the mother and calf is very, very strong.

They are also very intelligent. They have a fierce eye. If you are bringing them up the road from one field to another and they spot something, they may not go to it immediately but when you're gone they will come back. It might be some nice bit of fresh grass that they haven't spotted before. They'll be back.

I believe that they feel pain. They make a noise different to lowing; it's more like a moan. It might be because they stumbled over something and hurt themselves. When something like that happens, I really think they have greater healing powers than humans. One or two of them might have a cut and I put a spray on it, but in a short time it's all healed up. They are better than we are at healing, I think.

Sometimes, they go rambling. I can remember once noticing they were missing. Near my house there's an old bog road that goes onto a main road that leads to an abbey. I went looking for them. They had got in off the road in a mountain area with a lake at the bottom of it. They were just lying there and they seemed to have been eating heather, which they like. But it is rare for them to do that.

I've been very lucky, through all the years I've had the cows, in that I never had a situation where the herd had to be destroyed because of brucellosis, TB or anything like that. They've never been rejected after tests, either. That's partly because of the way

I keep them. I look after them well. I never had to get them a vet, only for the annual test.

I think part of the reason they are so healthy is that I followed the advice of a woman from Connemara. She had a great love of donkeys, goats, hens and all sorts of animals. She used always talk about donkeys and say that when you have one running with a herd of cattle you never have to have a vet. My cows are the proof of that, because I keep donkeys with them.

The donkeys and cows really get on together. If I put my donkeys in one field and the cows in another, there's all hell to pay, but if they are together they are fine. If they are in separate fields, the cows would be lowing because the donkeys are not in with them; they might be thinking that the donkeys got a better deal than they did. If they are together, everything is fine and there never is a health problem.

It can be a sad time when you have to get rid of an old cow that you've had for years. I remember, once, a man told me he would buy an old cow I had and bring her to the factory. We had such a difficulty getting her into the trailer. She obviously knew something was going to happen. She sensed it. It was very sad and upsetting.

I also remember when my mother died, back in 1990, we had her wake here in the house. On the evening of the removal, in the last few days of February, it was snowing and the cows were at the gate and they never stopped lowing. They knew there was something happening. She had a great love of animals, too, and they could sense that. They were all lined up at the gate. It was very moving.

It leads me to believe that all animals, including cows, are next to human. A lot of people in the West of Ireland have two or three of them. At one time, they kept them for milk and butter, but that day is gone. They still keep them to support their livelihood, but they are really pets for me.

I'm living on my own and I regard them as companions. They are so intelligent, just like humans; they just have different ways of communicating. They radiate love, at least to me, and I'm very fond of them. I have a great love for them and they radiate it back in so many different ways.

**MICHAEL describes his love for his nine pet snakes.**

There's something about snakes that not everyone likes. A lot of people get grossed out at even the thought of them. Many people won't touch them. They seem to think that they are going to be slimy. However, a lot of my friends who have seen them realise that their scales are quite smooth and they end up holding them and loving them. They hold them loose and the snakes explore wherever they want to go.

They love going for warmth, so they like to wrap themselves around you and hide in your clothing. The very first one I got is most interesting in that respect. Whenever you are holding him, within two minutes he goes up your sleeve and rests under your arm. He always heads for your sleeve. He would have a sleep up there. He's the only snake I have ever known who does that.

I decided to get my first snake when I was living with my ex-girlfriend. I had to get her agreement, but for the first few weeks she refused to hold him. She felt he was too scary and would bite her. It took me ages, months and months, to convince her that he wouldn't. Eventually, she decided to give it a go. Within five minutes, he went to the toilet on her. It freaked her out!

At first, she just froze in horror. After I cleaned up the mess, she ran straightaway for a shower. I couldn't stop laughing. We eventually got a few snakes and she grew to like looking at them but didn't like holding them. I suppose, appropriately, she is my ex, although our breakup occurred about six months later and over a different issue.

I also remember another friend who arrived over to my flat some time ago. For a while, she was afraid, too. By then, I had a four-foot snake. The four-footer can look big and menacing. I had bought her online off a guy, along with a tank and accessories, for one euro, which was a crazy bargain. At first, the snake was very nervous. It turned out that she hadn't been properly looked after or fed. I took care of her and she settled down quite quickly. She blossomed and opened up.

I had to convince my friend that this four-foot snake is very cuddly and lovable. After handling it a few times, she grew to love it. Unfortunately, the snake is very adventurous and likes going through people's hair. A couple of times, I had to disentangle it from her hair. It freaked her out, at first, but she ended up seeing the funny side of it.

I now have nine pet snakes ranging in age from about six months to four years, with three of them being males and the rest of them females. Their names are Mika, Zeek, Snowy, Roxy, Crystal, Rex, Eva, Drako and Kyra. They vary from about nine inches to my biggest which, as I mentioned, is four feet in length. They all have their own colours and patterns.

I wanted to go for unusual names and that's what I did. Sometimes, it would take me days to find a name that fits their character. All the snakes are different. Some are a bit snappy. Others are just plain lovely and like the attention; they are outward-going and love to explore. Others like to keep to themselves and are a bit shy and nervous; they often stay in their bedding and try to hide. More are very sneaky and try to escape a lot. So they all have very different characteristics and personalities, and I think that is reflected in the names.

They can bite, although only three of them have bitten me on purpose. Once a month, their eyes literally go blue, which is an indication that within a few days they are going to shed their skin. During that time, they become very timid and don't like being touched. I was trying to clean out the tank of one snake whose eyes had gone blue. I had to pick him up. He bit me because he didn't know what was going on as he couldn't see right.

I was bitten by another when it was shedding and I was giving it a bit of a wash. That time, it bit me on the hand and latched onto my thumb and tried to swallow it. It got about halfway down the nail and then let go. The third occasion involved a young snake who is not used to being handled, but he will calm down when he grows and gets used to me.

I keep all the snakes in tanks and I never let them sleep in my bed. You should never do that. People have ended up going to the vet and saying, 'I don't know what is wrong with the snake but it has stopped eating for months and it's becoming as straight as a ruler.' That can happen when they are sleeping beside you. It means they are basically sizing you up to try and eat you. A number of bigger snakes have tried to do that, so you never let a snake sleep with you.

Otherwise, snakes are very lovable even if they don't give you that much physical attention. With a dog, you can give it a pat and it will woof or give you a lick. With a snake, they can't lick you because they don't have a very big tongue. Because of that, a lot of people don't see the point in having them. But they do what they can with what they have.

I love keeping them. They are most interesting and are very beautiful creatures. They are not the sort of pets that everyone would expect you to have. Each one is different, and they have really nice personalities. You have to spend a lot of time looking after them, so you build up a stronger bond than you would with cats or dogs.

They are genuinely lovable, and although they can be really expensive to keep they are worth it. They may not be the best at attracting women – that's an understatement – but if a girl said to me 'it's me or the snake,' I'd say 'no problem' and I would keep the snake! I could never let them go.

**JOHN O CONNOR cares for wild birds, stray cats and dogs, and even a fox.**

We always had animals when I was growing up at home. My mother would be minding cats and we always had a dog. We had a cottage on an acre, so we had cows, pigs and turkeys. Although we kept those farm animals for the table or for market, I was never into that.

It wasn't until 2005 that I looked after animals on my own. Two dogs strayed in to me – a Labrador and also a gundog. I advertised and I tried to find a place for them, but I had no success. I decided to keep them and started to walk them every morning and evening. I found it very therapeutic.

They were great company. I would often go down to the shed and read while the dogs would be looking at me. I walked them around the fields. It was interesting to observe them. They might fight, but they'd be licking each other two seconds later. Forgiveness is a natural instinct to them. They eventually died, but I have kept other dogs since.

I started feeding birds, as well. I'd feed chaffinches, sparrows, robins and blackbirds from feeders at home. I'd also feed wild birds in the fields. The farmers' fields are surrounded by wooden fences with wooden poles about three inches wide at the top. I started putting broken peanuts on the top of the posts and finches would eat them up. The crows would eat the bread I'd bring for them.

Eventually, a flock of birds would be waiting for me. There would be chaffinches, blue tits, and robins in their own territory. There would be crows and magpies and little collared doves, one with a foot turned backwards. They would be there each morning and they'd follow me along.

The birds would move with me from post to post to post. They'd even follow me if I headed into the middle of a field. My brother was walking with me recently and he said, 'Those bloody birds! I thought they'd take the eye out of me!'

They have their own traits and personalities. The robins are very territorial and they would be in their own part of the field, except in the winter when there might be two or three together. The robin can be very cheeky. On one occasion, a robin even ate out of my hands, but that was on a very cold, frosty morning and it hasn't happened since.

The finches are gregarious and always together. The wagtails tend to pair off. The wren is very shy. The rook or magpie will just wait and come sneaking in. The old crows can get quite friendly. Unfortunately, some birds are gone – for example, I haven't heard the corncrake for donkey's years.

The one thing I love watching is starlings. They are brilliant the way they move together. I watch them in the evening and they'd be diving and soaring and twisting yet they'd never crash into each other. I think they behave the way a therapist would like to see a family of people behave. We should all be moving in the same direction, working in tandem and going with the flow. We have a lot to learn from starlings.

It's wonderful to watch birds feeding their young. I leave food on the ground for the smaller birds. You'll see the mammies picking up the food and putting it into their little mouths. Eventually, they stand back and let them at it themselves. Crows can be bigger than their mammies when they are babies, yet the mammies will feed them. They also stand back eventually as if to say, 'Come on. You can do it yourself.' The instinct they have is marvellous.

I also cared for a homing pigeon. It got knocked down on the road. I brought it in and fixed up its wing, and it stayed around. I had the pigeon for about seven years, but then it died. I also had a fox coming into the yard and it would practically feed out of my hand. It used to come along a few times each day and it was a bit fussy about the food it ate.

The fox would eat with the cats I keep. I have about 14 cats coming and going. I look after them as strays. I picked one up on the road as a kitten and had to wean her on a bottle. I got others that were brought to me. There are lots of strays because farmers introduce them to their fields to reduce the rabbit population but then they don't feed them and they arrive to me. They come and they go.

I believe that animals are best left in their natural habitat, although I don't mind people who keep tamed pets. I don't try to keep them or tame them. I would never have a budgie in the house, for example. Apart from the dogs and a few semi-tame cats, I let them stay on their own. I like to leave them with their independence and provide an open door if they need it.

Over time, I have become much more aware of birds and nature. Basically, I'm a wildlife person. I like the outdoor life. I might spend the winter indoors looking out, but I like to spend the summer outside looking in. It suits me and I love it. You're living in the now.

I feel I'm connecting with all the birds and animals. Someone said you should never do anything unless you do it for somebody else. I feel we're here to serve rather than be served. So I consider animals to be another family and I feel the need to help them. I really think we should give them more regard.

**DES HALL reflects on the use of teamwork and cooperation by birds. This is not a story about any particular pet but of two brilliant creatures and their search for food.**

Did you ever hear of somebody being birdbrained? Birds aren't supposed to have any brains at all, are they? Well, I remember looking out of my kitchen window, one morning, at the river beside my house. An otter was coming across the river. Normally, they dive down and then come up and chew something. But this otter was just swimming purposefully along.

I looked carefully and saw he had a fish in his mouth. It was a nice fish, but he wasn't eating it because it was too big to eat in the water. He was just taking it to the shore. He came up at the quay, put the fish down and started to eat it. I was looking at him, not thinking and not prepared for what I was about to see.

The next thing, two magpies stood in front of the otter. One of them stepped up to the fish and took a snap at it, but he got snapped back and he backed away. The other one then stepped forward to see if he could get a peck of fish, but he was snapped at, too. The two magpies stood back, turned around and looked at each other. They were clearly wondering what to do.

One of them then went around behind the otter, grabbed his tail and tweaked it. The otter swung around and had a snap at him. Once he did, the other magpie in front of the otter nipped in and got the first bite of the fish. They then reversed roles. They both did it twice, so they each had two bites of the fish.

The otter then swung back again and there were two magpies in front of him. Honest to God, I could almost see the two ears growing on the otter until they looked like an ass's two ears. It was like he was thinking, 'Who is the ass around here?' He then grabbed the fish, turned around, walked down the steps and took the fish back into the river. The two magpies then stepped up and tidied up after the otter, like good Christians should do for the TidyTowns Competition! The two of them had a damn good breakfast from the fish.

That story brings to mind a time when I saw a duck on the far slip of the river trying to get her brood from the nest down into the water. A magpie wanted one of them for breakfast. The duck was fighting the magpie off. Every time the magpie came down, the duck was there. She was hustling the brood into the water while fighting off the magpie. In the end, she got them all in and the magpie got nothing to eat.

I was telling that story to a chap the same day. I was describing how there's fierce puff in ducks when they are threatened and how that particular duck won. He asked me, 'Was there one magpie or two?' I said there was one. He said, 'If there were two, there wouldn't have been a duckling left!' Magpies really are brilliant creatures.

# TAILS OF THE UNEXPECTED

Animals have been known to do strange, inexplicable things. Most of us have heard of Greyfriars Bobby, the Skye Terrier who sat by his master's grave in Edinburgh for 14 years until his own death in 1872. Less widely known is the story of Canelo, a dog who waited outside a hospital in the Spanish city of Cádiz for 12 years for his master to emerge. The wait was in vain, however, as the owner had died shortly after being admitted; the dog died in 2002.

A nursing-home cat named Oscar became equally famous in 2007 for his ability to sense when patients were about to die; he would curl up with them shortly before they passed away. Another animal – a collie named Bobbie – travelled over 2,500 miles to his American master's home after being lost in 1923. Similar mysterious tales, involving dogs, a cat and horses, are recounted in the following pages.

**TOM CURRAN describes how, in the early 1960s, a horse named Linsey made a great escape from his family's farm in County Waterford.**

My father, who was a farmer at the time, bought the horse from the Travelling community. She was a lovely skewbald horse, very quiet, with reddish-brown and white markings and a sort of star on her forehead. She was friendly and easy to handle.

He had bought her as a workhorse and she served us for 18 years.

She was a really good worker. We had no tractor in those days, so she did a lot of the work on the farm. We used to have a few acres of beet and she would pull it on the cart down to the road for collection by the lorries. She would plough, harrow and open drills. You need a good, steady animal to open drills, to keep them straight, and she was good at that.

We called her Linsey and we took care of her very well. She had her own stable next to the cow byre. We would feed her hay and oats. We would also feed her mangels, which were like sugar beet. In the summertime, she would have to be clipped; we used to use hand clippers to do that. She had a good life.

One morning, after about ten years, my father went out to the field and she was gone. It must have been summertime. We searched all over Ring and Old Parish, in as far as Dungarvan, which is about seven miles away. We informed the guards and checked all the fields, every place. We saw no sign of her. She had never done this before, but she was definitely gone. We thought she must have been stolen.

My dad put an ad in the local paper in Dungarvan, describing Linsey. He gave the number of the post office in Ring because, like a lot of people, we had no phone back then. After a couple of days, a call arrived from near Clonmel telling us that they believed they had our horse. They said that she had just rambled into their farm. We were amazed because the place was about 30 miles away from where we lived.

Two local young men, who were friends of my father and had worked sometimes for him, cycled up to the farm near Clonmel. They knew the horse well. Like everybody else, they thought, 'This is a long shot because it's so far away.' The moment they went into the farmyard, they knew straightaway that it was Linsey. She probably recognised them, too, because she was a very cute horse.

The two men brought her home. They got a rope and tied it around her neck, and she followed them. They cycled home, with one of them behind her and the other in front. I don't think anyone had cars or other transport in Ring in those days. We were really delighted to see her. I remember being particularly pleased because I was so young.

We were all amazed. We wondered, 'How could she have gone so far?' To even make it into Dungarvan would have been difficult, never mind travelling on to near Clonmel. There were lots of bad roads back then, along with hills and mountains. Even though she was well-shod, to have set off in the evening and got so far was extraordinary. She also had no food and maybe decided to turn into the farmyard to see if she could find something to eat.

About eight years later, when she was 18, the same thing happened. She was out grazing in the fields and it got dark. Dad went out the next day looking for her and she was gone. She must have left early again. We searched everywhere – no luck. We rang the last people who had found her near Clonmel – no luck, either. A fortnight went by and there was still no sign of Linsey. She had disappeared.

Seeing that she had headed towards Clonmel before, this time my dad decided to put an ad in one of the Clonmel papers. After about a week, a phone call came to Ring post office. It was from a lady called Mrs. le Terrier from Kiltinan Castle, Fethard, County Tipperary. She told us she had Linsey.

Yet again, we couldn't understand how Linsey had got so far, especially through or around Clonmel and over the bridge to head for Fethard. It was about 40 miles away and a very tough journey. How did she get through Dungarvan and Clonmel? That was two times she had tried it. It was very strange.

This time, another man went up. He had a motorbike. I went with him, sitting on the back. We collected a saddle from friends of ours and brought it with us. I was about 14 or 15 at the time and I had never been on a saddle in my life. We headed off for Fethard.

We arrived at the castle. There were so many different types of animals around. The man I was with knocked at the door and the woman came out. 'Are you Mrs. Tarrier?' he asked, mispronouncing her name. 'Yes, I am Mrs. le Terrier,' she said. She then brought us off to Linsey and told us what had happened.

She explained how Linsey had rambled in the gate of the castle and walked up around to where the other horses were. They were in what was like a corral or a field. Linsey was just standing there. Mrs. le Terrier had recognised her instantly.

She said she had sold Linsey to the Travellers 18 years before. She used to do a lot of business with them, buying and selling. She knew her markings since the time she had sold her. Mrs. le Terrier knew immediately that she had come home.

We had a cup of tea and a chat with Mrs. le Terrier. We then put the saddle on Linsey. It was probably the first time a saddle was ever on her. I hopped up and off we went home with the motorbike ahead and me behind.

After a while, the motorcyclist went back down to Ring and returned bringing my brother Paud with him. He and I swapped places, and I went home. I was exhausted. My brother brought her back the rest of the way. We didn't get home until evening and we were all very tired. It was like *Into the West.*

We went down to the stable one morning, not long after, and she had died. My dad cried when he saw her. We dug a hole out in the field and we buried her there, on the land. The boys who had been involved in getting her back from Fethard were there, too. It was very sad.

She had been a great horse, very special. I suppose, looking back, she must have known she was going to die soon and she wanted to get back home to where she was bred. That's why she made those two trips, the second one successfully. It was extraordinary. She was a very special horse. She had gone home to where she was bred and walked in to where she was born. And that was the story of Linsey. I'll never forget her.

**CAMILLA MC CARTHY tells of a very strange event surrounding her husband's death and the family dog Toby.**

Toby was a black Labrador with a wonderful personality. He was like a politician. He would greet everybody, one after the other. He would start with the first person and go through everybody until each and every person was greeted. For Toby, however, my husband Jim was always number one.

We got him in 1996, when he was a puppy. He was a slim dog, jet-black with a sort of narrow face and beautiful big eyes. He was very silky and with a face full of expression. We had lost our last Labrador from heart failure. My husband was very big into dogs and he wanted another. He got Toby from his first cousin, and the dog took to Jim straightaway.

Jim was farming and I was out working, so he was with Jim all day. Toby went everywhere with him, all over the farm. Jim had a workshop where he fixed all sorts of electronic things and Toby would sit in there with him. They would come in at ten o'clock for tea, he'd get a biscuit and they'd go off out again. Everywhere Jim went, Toby would be with him, except when he came walking with me.

Jim trained Toby to do everything. If you said, 'Get your lead,' he'd go out and get his lead; 'Go get my cap' and he'd get the cap and bring it back in; 'Get my boots' and he'd fetch the boots. If I said, 'Get my runners,' which I'd use for walking, he'd bring in the runners. Jim even had him trained to pick up letters that came through the post box and bring them in.

He was so intelligent, it was unbelievable. He was so bright that you could take him for a walk without being on a lead. If a car came, he'd sit back alongside you in at the dike at the edge of the road and wait for the car to pass. People would stop and ask, 'Does he really always do that?' But he wasn't just bright; he was also affable and affectionate. He'd put the paw up to you and lie at your feet.

Eventually, in 1999, Jim got leukaemia and he was in hospital for six weeks. I think the dog was aware that something was going on. He didn't see Jim for all that time, and he didn't see me for three weeks of it. He could see that I was quite traumatised by what was happening, as well.

The night before Jim was transferred to hospital in Dublin, he asked his best friend Tony, 'Will you look after the dog for me?' Tony was a friend from his schooldays. He said, 'I will, of course, Jim.' The dog was the most important thing to Jim. He adored him. Then, after only six weeks, Jim died.

Toby was affected by the death. He would arrive down to the bedroom looking for Jim. He would wander around the house trying to find him. Sometimes, if he heard a noise outside, he would whine. If he heard footsteps, he might think it was Jim and then realise it wasn't. He started jumping up on Jim's chair. Anything he could see that might belong to Jim, he tried to get it.

After Jim's death, I visited his grave every day, which was about two miles away, but I never brought Toby with me. I didn't want to bring a dog into a graveyard out of respect for the graves, if nothing more. I wouldn't want a dog running over them. So Toby never came there with me.

Two or three months after Jim died, however, I went up to Galway for a family event. I was away for two days. When I came back down, the dog didn't want to leave me out of his sight. He wanted to be with me all the time. Because of that, when I decided to visit Jim's grave, I said, 'I'll take Toby with me.'

When we got to the graveyard, I opened the car door. Before I could stop him, Toby jumped out. He looked back at me as I was locking the door of the car. He then ran ahead of me and went straight to Jim's grave and sat at it. He had gone directly to the right grave. That's the one he had singled out. There was no rambling; it was just straight down to the correct place.

Jim's grave was probably a couple of hundred yards from the car. It was a long way away. There was a path down the centre, with graves on either side, and the grave was around 14 headstones away. Yet Toby had headed straight for it and had sat down immediately he got there.

It was very strange what happened. I just couldn't believe it. I was amazed. I wondered, 'Is it just a coincidence?' I then fixed the flowers and said a few prayers. After that, I said, 'Come on, Toby, we'll go home.' He turned and came with me and got into the car. And that was it.

I couldn't get my head around what Toby had just done. I wondered, 'Was it something that he sensed?' or 'Did he sense from me where I was about to go?' Obviously, he had got some sense of something but I couldn't understand what it could be. It certainly said something about the connection between the three of us – Jim, Toby and I – and particularly the connection between Jim and the dog.

About two months later, Toby started to lose the hair on his legs. Patches started appearing. I thought it might have been caused by a tick, or something, so I brought him to a vet. They tried all sorts of things, but they didn't work. Eventually, I changed to another vet. I walked in to him and explained what the problem was.

He turned to me and asked, 'Has anything happened to the dog in his life in the last few months?' I said, 'He was my husband's dog and my husband died some months ago.' He said, 'That's your problem, the dog is grieving. He is grieving for your husband and picking up your grief.' He told me it was affecting him and that was the reason for the loss of hair.

He also said to me, 'If you don't mind yourself, as well, you'll be like the dog. You don't look too good, either.' He was a very nice, concerned man. He recommended natural remedies like drops and ointments and things like that. 'I can't guarantee that the dog's hair will grow back again, but hopefully we'll be able to stop it being lost,' he told me.

The hair did grow back again and, from that day on, Toby picked up. After that, he grew very attached to me and to my husband's friend Tony. Tony would call up and see that the dog was alright and I was alright. He took Jim's request literally. He and his wife were very good both to me and Toby.

The second year after Jim died, Toby was still affected by what had happened. I was going away for a few days and I had packed my suitcase. I had left it down in the spare bedroom.

The phone rang and I went down to answer it. When I came back up, wasn't he after taking several things out of my case. He had them up in the kitchen and he was lying on them. It was as if he was saying, 'I don't want you to go.' It got to the stage that when I was going on holidays, I'd have to hide the case.

Toby lived a long life and was 16 and a half when he died. I buried him with my husband's cap. The reason I did that was because I had left my husband's cap hanging up in the utility room. If the cap fell down when somebody was taking a coat down, he would take the cap, bring it into the kitchen, and I'd see him lying on it there. He did that for years after Jim died. He never forgot. So when Toby died, I buried him with the cap. I thought, 'The two of you go together!' He was just a beautiful dog, he really was.

**Tom Brennan explains how he owes everything to a wonderful dog called Rex.**

My story dates back to the early 1950s, when I was a very small toddler and just beginning to crawl. We lived in a small housing estate at the time. Our house was in a part of the estate that was complete, but there was a lot of building going on up the road. As a result, trucks would be travelling up and down all day, bringing materials to the site.

One sunny day, my mother put me out near the front door, lying on a blanket. The door looked down along a path to the gates below. The path must have been ten feet long. Outside the gates was a road. A lorry had just passed up the road and, because it was a fine day, there was a cloud of dust.

Apparently, I crawled to the gate and crawled out through the bars. There was probably a foot separating each of the bars, which I worked my way through. I was sitting in a cloud of dust, in the middle of the road, just as another lorry was coming along.

At that time, we owned a black German Shepherd called Rex. He saw what was happening, cleared the gate, caught me by my nappy and pulled me back to the side of the road. The lorry driver saw him and stopped. He came in to my mother and told her that the dog had cleared the gate and pulled me out of the dust. 'I'd have killed your child only for that dog,' he said. 'Because of the dust, I would never have seen him.'

Later that day, things had eased up on the building site and I was put out in the yard again. I was by the front door. Rex was in the yard, too. A neighbour who was a friend of my mother came to visit. Didn't the dog savage her in the yard! It seems he was looking after me again. That's what my father believed, anyway.

The neighbour was a very nice woman, with a heart of gold, but Rex had done a lot of damage to her legs. There was murder over what had happened. My father came home from work and pleaded with the woman not to take any action. He told her about what the dog had done for me earlier in the day.

Because my father didn't want Rex to be destroyed, he gave him away that same day. He gave him to a farmer who lived nearby, across a few fields. The farmer seemingly told my father that, to begin with, he would tie the dog up in the yard and keep him like that until he got used to the place. Then he'd start walking him and letting him run free.

That same day, however, coming up to around twilight, Rex broke loose and started to run towards home. He ran through the fields and headed for the main road. He jumped a stile near where we lived, hit the grass margin and rolled out onto the road. At that moment, he was killed by the same truck that he had saved me from earlier that day!

What happened was very strange, indeed. I remember telling the story to the artist Walter Verling, who remarked, 'That's the balance of the universe – a life for a life.' It's hard to find the meaning of it, but it certainly affected my father. After that, for many years, he refused to have a dog in the house.

My father changed his mind when I was about eight or nine years old. A travelling funfair came to the area and they had a guard dog. He was a vicious thing, coloured black and tan. Being a young boy, I ran straight over to the dog and threw my arms around him. The woman who owned the funfair came running out, screaming. She thought the dog would savage me, but he didn't touch me.

My grandmother used to supply the funfair with electricity to run the chair-o-planes and things like that. She used to give them water, as well. They must have had a chat and the decision was made that when the funfair left, the dog would stay with me. It seems, by that stage, he wouldn't go with them.

He was pretty old when I got him and I only owned him a couple of years, but he became my best friend. Everywhere I went, he went with me. His name was Dandy. I was no good at playing football, but when I played with the other lads the dog would run over to the ball and sit on it. He would let no one near it until I got it.

Nobody could take the ball off him. If the ball was in the air, he'd run to it and catch it in his mouth. Then he'd lie down on the field until I came up to collect it. None of my friends would play with me because of the dog. They had to ban me from playing football, as a result.

Although I'm not a great dog lover now, and I don't have any at home, if I got one it would have to be a German Shepherd. I think that's because of Rex. My mother and father both told me the story about him so many times over the years. They might start saying something to me like, 'It's a miracle you are here because .......' Then they'd tell me what happened.

The story is still vivid in my mind. As a child, it didn't mean much to me, but as I have got older I realise the potential consequence of what happened. If Rex hadn't pulled me back that day, I wouldn't have married, had children or grandchildren. You could say that all the things that are as a consequence of my existence are down to that caring dog called Rex.

**DES HALL reflects on the extraordinary sixth sense of horses, as exemplified by the experience of a horse owned by his uncle.**

My uncle always had a horse. He wasn't a wealthy man, but the horse would have the best of oats and the finest of hay. He used to keep the horse in a field behind the house. He didn't bother bringing it in during the winter. Instead, he would bring a bit of a meal out to it in the evening. Even when the weather would be fairly rough, the horse would be OK.

This day, the weather ahead was looking nasty. My uncle heard what he thought was a hell of a kicking noise at the gate to the field. He looked out and there was the horse kicking the gate. He went out to see what was wrong. While he was there, the horse kicked the gate again. My uncle opened the gate and the horse walked past him, went into the yard and up to the stable door.

The horse then kicked the stable door. My uncle opened it and the horse walked in and turned around. That was that, and no more was said. My uncle put some water into the bucket and the feed was put into the manger. He was left wondering, 'What was that all about?'

My uncle went to bed that night and a huge storm blew up. In the morning, he woke up and looked out into the yard. All seemed right. The horse was looking out over the stable door, smiling at him. He then looked into the field and three ash trees had come down in the field during the night!

My uncle was later talking to his vet and telling him about what a clever horse he had and how he demanded to be brought in when the weather was going contrary. The vet said, 'He was intelligent. He wanted to get in out of the weather because he knew the trees were coming down!'

The vet then said, 'I'll tell you a better one.' He described how he kept horses and how he and his family used to bring them in every night. 'We always stable them,' he said. He then said that on that same night of the storm they had gone out in the ordinary way to get the horses, but instead of coming in they were away in the far side of the field. 'We went after them, to catch them,' he said, 'but they ran around us in small circles and we couldn't get them.'

He said, 'We offered them food and bits of oats, you name it, but they still ran circles around us. In the end, we just said, "Oh! To hell with them! They can stay out here and freeze."' He said they left the field, shut the gate, went in and closed the door.

They woke up in the morning, looked out, and there were the horses looking over the gate of the field and smiling. He then looked at the stable – the storm had blown it flat!

**AOIFE ROSE O'BRIEN talks about her extraordinary childhood connection with Bran, the family dog. This is a story of life and death from the mid-1990s.**

When I was about three months old, my mom bought an Irish Wolfhound. We were almost the same age. He had been born on 9 July 1992, four days after me. He was huge, with a deep-grey coat, a sort of silver-and-grey mix. They called him Bran and he was the biggest pet ever, absolutely gorgeous.

For some reason, he took to me from day one. He developed a big connection with me and he never left my side. I was the favourite. I was his world. If I was taking a nap or my mother was feeding me – whatever I was doing – he was with me.

People have told me I could poke him in the eye and he'd never even bat an eyelid. I would pull his ear and he'd sit there wagging his tail. My mom has told me I'd be putting my finger in his mouth or touching his teeth.

I would pull his tail or, when I started walking, I'd climb up on his back. He loved it. He'd sit there for hours on end and let me do what I wanted, but if anybody else went near him he'd get cross with them.

When I was only 12 months old, I started having epileptic fits. When I had my very first fit, Bran was the one who alerted my parents. I was upstairs, asleep in my cot, and he was beside me. He noticed straightaway. He started barking like crazy and he went and got my parents. My mother came up and saw what was happening.

Once the seizures started, they developed very fast. I had a couple of seizures in the first month or two. As a result, I was in and out to the doctor a lot. We lived down a really long lane out in the countryside. The lane was about 500 metres long and it joined up with a back road down at the end. Anytime I would leave the house to go to the doctor, he would sit at the end of the lane and refuse to move until I came home.

My parents would try to put Bran into the back of the car and bring him back to the house, but he would go crazy and get out again and go back down to the end of the lane. He'd also refuse to eat until I arrived home. When he'd see the car coming, even though he wouldn't know I was in it, he'd get up and start wagging his tail.

I had to go up to hospital in Dublin for two or three weeks, where they did a lot of tests. Everybody was puzzled because the scans and tests didn't show signs of epilepsy, but I was still having epileptic fits. During that time, Bran refused to stay in the house; instead, he stayed the whole time at the end of the lane. My parents started to get really worried. They were afraid he was getting too upset.

When I came home, I was very sick so I wasn't able to crawl or be outside with Bran very much. I would be in the sitting-room and he would lie down beside me. If I made one bit of a sound or one tiny movement, he'd be straight up watching me and wondering if everything was OK, or barking for my mom.

Eventually, I started getting better, but what was strange was that Bran started getting sick. I was about one and a half or two at that stage. My mom brought the vet out to him and he did a lot of tests. He told her that Bran was showing signs of epilepsy. He went on medication straightaway, but it didn't work.

For the next eight or nine months, as I got better he got worse. I was taken off medication and was seizure-free, but he was getting seizures nearly every day. The fits seemed to have been quite scary, especially because he was so big. They went

161

on for a lot longer than mine, about five or 10 minutes. I was told that as soon as he got a fit, I'd start crying.

Because I was still recovering and he was sick, he ended up staying in with me all the time. He used to sleep beside me and stay with me. I can see that from every photo I have of me from that time; he's either right beside me or under my feet.

Then, when I was about three, Bran died from epilepsy. My parents buried him out in our back garden. For years and years after, when I was younger, anytime I was upset I'd bring him flowers and sit by his grave and talk to him. I didn't physically remember him because I had been so young when he was alive, but I knew he had such an impact on my life that he was still my best friend.

What happened was absolutely insane. Our connection was so strong. Many people have said that he must have been my guardian angel. He was there in the background watching over me and then he died from epilepsy himself.

My parents thought that what happened was amazing, too. They told me the story time and time again as I grew up. I also heard the story told by so many other people. Nearly every neighbour or friend of my parents, or anyone else, they all remember the connection between Bran and me. So it wasn't just my parents telling me; it was other people, too.

They have all commented on what happened to me so many times. They saw my seizures and Bran's seizures, and they also saw his behaviour with me. Every one of them thought that the connection was absolutely incredible. A lot of people might say what happened was only coincidence, but I don't think so because our connection was so powerful from day one.

I've also had many close encounters in my life. When I was 14, I fractured my neck after an awful fall from a horse. I was paralysed for a few hours and tore the ligaments in my leg. Everyone said I should have died. I've also been in a very bad car crash, where the car has been totalled but I've come out of it with a few cuts and bruises. So many people have said it's because Bran is looking after me.

Today, Bran is still part of my life. I have pictures of him in my house, and the story of him always comes up especially if we have a few people around for dinner or we are in the pub having a few drinks at weekends. Some people will always get me to tell the story of Bran again. So, although I'm 23 now, I will never forget him. I may not remember him physically, but I still have the memory of an extraordinary dog who was a best friend to me when I was unwell as a child.

JODIE **inherited her deceased father's dog and was soon witnessing a strange event at his graveside.**

Nippy was a Labrador cross and had a brown eye and a pale-blue eye. He was a really friendly, loveable dog, and he followed my father Paddy everywhere. Once Daddy retired, he started a garden with tomatoes and marrows and those sorts of things. He would be in the garden first thing in the morning and the dog would be with him.

Daddy would wear a sleeveless jacket to keep him warm and in the pocket he'd have dog biscuits. Nippy would just go over and help himself whenever he felt like it. They got on really well and they were the best of friends. They did everything together. Nippy never left his side.

Eventually, my dad became unwell. He had emphysema and had to use oxygen. When I'd go in to see him, Nippy would be with him. He would be sitting beside the bed with his head on the pillow, looking straight at my dad. Daddy would be having conversations with him and it looked like Nippy was able to understand every word he was saying.

Unfortunately, my dad died and my mother didn't feel able to look after Nippy. She wasn't an animal person. She rang the vet and asked, 'Will you come and take him?' He ended up with the vet. I didn't want anything happening to him, so we went up to the vet's to find out what was going on.

Nippy was ecstatic to see us. When we were outside talking, we could hear him barking inside. He was going mental. Our son was sitting in the backseat of the car, which was one of those cars with a sliding passenger door in the back. We had left the door open. The vet opened the cage to let the dog out. He went like a bullet, straight out and into the car.

I don't know how he knew it was our car because he had never been in it before. There were other cars in the car park, yet he headed straight to ours. He was actually crying when he got into the car. He was so excited it was like he was talking to us. We had brought him some dog biscuits and he was thrilled with them, too.

That first night at home, we left him down in the kitchen and we went upstairs to bed. My parents' house was one storey, but we had two storeys. I woke up in the night to find the dog with his head on the pillow beside me and his face looking into my eyes. He had never been on a stairs before, to my knowledge, and it was pitch-dark.

He quickly made himself at home. He would get up on the couch and stretch out full-length. He could sit where he liked, which he wasn't used to. He'd put his head on a cushion. We also spoiled him with the doggie biscuits, which we continued to give him. We couldn't punish him by not letting him have what he was used to. He seemed very happy to be with us.

We went over, a few days later, to visit my father's grave and we brought the dog with us. He had never been there before. He hadn't been involved in the funeral arrangements or anything like that. When we were going into the graveyard, we left the dog off the leash. He didn't go near the other graves close to us. He just headed straight on.

He first went down past maybe ten, 11 or 12 rows of graves. My father's grave was even further away than that, in a new section through a gap in the wall. He went through the gap, too. When we got there, Nippy was lying full-length on my father's grave. He had gone straight to the correct place even though he didn't know where to go.

He kept looking at the grave and you could see the sadness in his eyes. He was whining a bit, also. When we were coming home, he left his calling card all around the grave. He did his wee everywhere by the graveside. It didn't surprise me because he and my father were such great pals.

I could see in the weeks that followed that Nippy was heartbroken after my father's death. He'd look at you really sad. You could see his soul through his eyes, and he was totally lost and pining. I really believe he was heartbroken that his master had gone.

Nippy was only with us a matter of months when he got cancer. He developed a huge lump in his stomach. He was about 12 years old at the time. You could see he was in pain. We had to get him put down because he would have suffered, and we couldn't have that.

It's bad enough if a human is in pain; at least they can tell you. But animals can't tell you how they are feeling or what they need. So I believe that we were right to do what we did. It was sad to lose him, and his death marked the end of an era for me. It was like having to let go all over again after the death of my dad.

**The following is the experience of EDEL, who believes that the soul of Pixie, her deceased cat, came to say goodbye.**

We were just married and living in a very old house. It is 200 years old and had a problem with 'furry friends'. I said, 'We'll get two kittens.' We got the name of a lady who takes in rescue kittens and we took two of them. We called them Pixie and Dixie. I think they were brother and sister. Pixie was the girl and Dixie the boy.

We brought them home and they settled in very well. I was never that much into cats, but after Pixie and Dixie arrived I became very fond of them. My husband was fond of them, too. In fact, he was always mad about cats. At that time, we had no children so they were a bit like twins in the house. Cats have a way of weaving themselves into your house and your relationships, and that's what they did. Everybody was happy.

One day, I was on my way home from work. I stopped about five miles from home and did some shopping. Afterwards, I got back in the car. I was driving away when my car filled with Pixie's smell. It was a very distinctive smell. It felt like she was in the car, to the point that I wondered should I pull over to see if she was in the boot.

Eventually, the smell left the car and I was approaching the house where we live. It is located at the bottom of a hill. When I got to the bottom, who was there only Pixie. She had been knocked over and was dead on the side of the road! I was in an awful state and phoned my husband. He said, 'I only left the house a very short time ago, and before I left I fed the two cats at the back of the house. She was alive then.' So I had got the smell around the same time that Pixie was killed.

I believe that Pixie had come to me to say goodbye. I had a definite sense of that. I thought she had come to say she was moving on. That point was reinforced that evening when I was going into town with my husband. He asked me, 'Do you get Pixie's smell in the car?' I couldn't get it then, but he got it. To me, that was really significant. He was really fond of the cat. I think Pixie had come to him, too.

I believe everything has a spark of life, a spark of the divine. The fact that we, as humans, believe we have that spark more than animals puts them in a very subordinate position. Instead, I think we all share the same air and we all have souls, including Pixie, and I also don't think any of us goes from this to nothingness. I think that's true whether you have a cat or mouse or little dog or whatever – we are all a spark of the divine.

I don't know if where we all end up will be in the form we currently know on this planet. I think it will be more like the Hindu concept that we're all a spark and we all gel in together as part of the Brahman, the bigger reality. So I don't know that when I pass on I'll see Pixie in a cat form, but we'll all be part of the one, whatever that 'one' is.

**MARGARET CASEY relates how the family dog lost the will to live after her husband became ill with cancer.**

We originally owned a stray golden Labrador we had taken in from the streets but the dog was poisoned and died. The girls in my family were devastated and my cousin promised them a pup. We ended up getting an Alsatian called Mac.

Everybody was mad about the dog. He was as placid as could be, a lovely dog. He would sit with you and lick you. My two daughters used to play with him. My husband would play with him, too. He would hop into my daughter's bed and ruin the duvet cover; she would turn it over so that you wouldn't notice it for a couple of days.

The girls used to cycle to school and he knew the time in the evening when they came home. He'd be outside the gate, sitting there, waiting for them. When they'd hit the end of our road, he would trot off to meet them and escort them home. He also used to greet other people he knew who came to visit.

He was the liveliest of dogs you could meet. The girls used to have a ball out on the lawn and they'd be flying around with him. It got so lively that, one day, one of them banged her head and nearly had to go to the doctor. If the birds were flying above him in the fields, he'd be chasing them and thinking he could fly.

The dog struck up a relationship with my husband, Liam, and followed him everywhere. He became closely attached to him. Liam was a carpenter and he owned a van and, from the very beginning, he brought the dog everywhere. The dog loved going off in the van. He used to sit on the front seat, as proud as punch, with his head up on Liam's shoulder.

Even if Liam was working out in the garage, the dog would be with him. They were always together. He would sit with Liam even when he was eating. They were a real pair. He was a one-man dog all of his life.

In January 1994, my husband started complaining of severe heartburn. He was in and out to the doctor getting all sorts of medicines. Then, one night, he got a desperate pain in his chest. I thought he was having a heart attack. He wasn't able to eat and he was getting weaker.

When they eventually checked him out in the hospital, they found he had stomach cancer. It was the worst form of stomach cancer you could get. They performed a five-hour operation and he had most of his stomach removed. He survived and eventually came out of hospital.

During that time, you could see a huge change in Mac. He picked up on what was happening and he knew that there was something wrong. He used to come into the bedroom, walk around the bed, sniff around, and then he'd walk back out. He'd lie down outside on the grass and not move. The girls said that Mac's eyes had gone sad. The tail would be down and the life went out of him.

My husband had a bench out in the garage, with a piece of carpet on top, and the dog used to lie on it. He did that when there was nobody around and he'd look out the garage window. He could see everything that was going on. After my husband got sick, he would no longer do that. Even if strangers came in, he'd just lie there and ignore everyone. He wouldn't bother with anything.

In July, Liam got bad again and went back into hospital. At that stage, they only gave him ten days to live. However, he rallied around and I got to bring him home. We took care of him from then until he died on 21 September. He was aged 53. That night, the dog howled.

Just after Liam died, Mac started to get worse. His back legs began to go. He was dragging his legs after him. He went completely downhill. In the end, he just gave up the ghost. We could see he was in pain and feeling miserable. By January, he was so bad that we had to get our next-door neighbour to bring up a vet and put him down. We buried him across the road. It was like another funeral.

I still have a photo of Mac in the kitchen. It's a photo Liam took of him and got blown up and framed. It is still there. It's where Liam hung it and I've never taken it down. It brings back memories of a lovely dog and a loyal friend to my husband.

Looking back, I definitely believe that Mac sensed what was happening. He knew everything that was going on. Liam was his master and he saw him going. There was nothing left for him. His friend was gone, and he was just so sad in the end.

**PATRICIA PLUNKETT explains how her dog's unusual barking foretold her uncle's death.**

Lassie was a black-and-white collie cross. He was actually my mum's dog. She had bought him as a pup. He loved my mother. Wherever she went – to the shops or bingo – the dog walked with her. When she was out without him, he would wait at the front door until she came home again. He was really loyal to my mother and she absolutely loved him.

He was so quiet and he would rarely bark. Because of that, he really wasn't cut out to be a watchdog. When my mother's house was broken into, the dog was in the kitchen and he didn't make a sound. The burglar was probably rubbing his head! The truth was that he could make friends with everybody.

Eventually, my parents retired and couldn't keep the dog anymore. It wasn't possible for them to do that where they were going to live. He was also on his last legs. I said, 'The dog is getting old, maybe it's time to put him down.' She said, 'No, no!' So I said, 'I'll mind him,' and I did. I lived only two miles away from where they were moving to and I told her she could come visit him anytime.

He was quite content when he came to stay with me. Even though we had another dog, he was happy. My mother would come out to visit him and he was always glad to see her. Things worked out pretty well. But he was still useless as a guard dog because he never barked.

That all changed at half past eleven one night. I was out in the kitchen trying to tune in a new television we had got that day. I was standing against the window. My husband was in bed because he had to get up early. I heard three bangs against the back door. The kids heard them, too. They were saying, 'Who's here at this hour of the night?'

I thought, 'Oh, my God! Who could that be outside?' I didn't want to go out. I wasn't going to open the door myself. I just looked out the window and I turned on the outside light. The only thing I thought of was that someone might have had an accident outside and was looking for a telephone or whatever.

The strange thing was that the dog was standing there and looking at the back door, barking away. He kept looking at the door. He had rarely barked, so I was drawn to him. You could see from the expression in his eyes that he was actually seeing something. I was 100 per cent sure there was somebody out there, but there wasn't.

I said to one of the children, 'Go down and get Dad.' My husband came up, went out, walked around the house, and there wasn't a sign of anybody. But the dog was still standing there, looking at the back door and barking. The other dog wasn't barking at all, which was unusual. I thought, 'This is odd!'

Eventually, the dog settled down. The kids went off to bed. And I went off to bed. However, 20 minutes later, at ten minutes to midnight, the dog started this unmerciful crying under my window. The dog never did that before. It really was an unmerciful howl. I said, 'There's something wrong! Someone is going to die!' I said it to my husband. He said, 'I don't know what is wrong with that dog. I have never heard him cry like that.'

I was so upset I didn't sleep. I was waiting for someone to ring to tell me that my mother or father had died. They lived in the town on their own. But nothing happened. However, at seven o'clock the next morning, the phone rang. I said, 'This is it!' I got up and answered it. It was my mother on the phone. She said, 'Your uncle died last night.' He was her brother. He had died of a heart attack. I thought, 'My God! I don't believe it!'

I eventually went over to the funeral in Manchester. I was talking to my cousins about what happened that night. I told them about everything that occurred. They asked me what time the dog had barked. I told them that he first barked at half past eleven. They said my uncle had dropped at the top of the stairs at half past eleven.

I then told them about the awful whining from the dog at ten minutes to midnight. They told me that was when my uncle had taken his last breath and died. An ambulance had come, but it was too late and he was declared dead. So the first time the dog barked was the exact time he had collapsed and the second time he barked was when my uncle had died. I found it all so extraordinary, especially considering that all this barking had come from the dog who never barked.

The dog only lived for a very short time after that, just a matter of days. We knew, at the time, that he wasn't going to live long because he was old, about 15 years of age. I often wondered, 'What am I going to do with him when he is dying?' But he actually went up the field and lay down and died. It all happened within days of my uncle's death. He had actually died before my uncle's funeral took place in England. It was like he had done his last duty.

I believe that we can all pick up energies and animals can do so, too. I especially believe that dogs have a great sensitivity about them. They can sense fear and lots of other things. I believe that if a person has an ulterior motive, a dog can pick it up. They can read a person better than another person can.

I think this dog could pick up what was happening to my uncle. I think my uncle's spirit was coming to me and the dog was aware of that. I think he sensed his spirit at the back door. I have absolutely no doubt it was him that night. He was coming to say goodbye and I have no doubt the dog sensed it. I thought it was all most remarkable.

# HELPFUL COMPANIONS

Irish author Pádraic Ó Conaire (1882 – 1928) spared nothing in extolling the virtues of donkeys. He did so in an amusing short story titled *My Little Black Donkey*. The tale depicts a dealer outrageously overstating the qualities of an animal Ó Conaire was attempting to buy.

The donkey was 'intelligent' and 'as innocent as the priest,' the dealer stressed. Give him a handful of oats once a month and no racehorse could keep up with him. He even once saved a drowning child. After much haggling, the price was set at one pound with an added sixpence for each child. It transpired there were lots of children!

Donkeys like Ó Conaire's have been part of the Irish rural landscape for many hundreds of years. They have worked on farms alongside horses and dogs. Dogs have also been invaluable to people with special needs – and even to one sporting hero – as you are about to read.

**PAT KENNEDY remembers Timmy, the workhorse on his family farm from well over half a century ago.**

Timmy was an old reddish-brown hunter. They were a special breed of horse, nearly a thoroughbred, extremely clever and would jump like hell. He was retired from hunting when we got him, around the early or mid-1950s, and he was with us until around 1963.

He was a big, powerful animal, about 16 hands tall. You could see the bloodlines shining on his neck. He wouldn't be like the hairy workhorse at all. He was more like a racehorse, but he was not fit for racing. Hunters generally would be good for nothing else only hunting, but this fellow could do anything.

He was initially left here just to graze around as a kind of pet, but my father soon found out that although he was around 20 or 24 years old he could work and was extremely clever. He would do scuffling and setting beet and setting mangels and all of that. You could put him under a dray or bring in hay with him. Anything that involved a small machine being behind him, he would do excellently.

Tractors were scarce then and horses like Timmy were vital. You'd have to be badly stuck to hire in a tractor; everything would be done by horse. Horses could do some things even better. When the tractor came in, you'd have compaction caused by the weight of the wheels on the ground. The ground becomes wicked hard, the rain sets in, and you have next to nothing. But when you would till with a horse, everything would be natural. You could do things with horses that you can't do now.

Timmy settled in well and he took to our place immediately. Although we had a stable, he would mostly be over around the fields. He would head over to the farmhouse if he felt there was something going on or he wanted a little bit of grub. He would walk along to the gate and look in at you. He would wait until you took notice of him.

He'd whinny at first, just to get your attention. He'd look at you and you'd have to figure out what he wanted. Generally what he wanted was grub. We'd normally give him a bit of oats or a mangel or a spud, and only then would he go away. We might also give him an apple or a carrot, which he loved – they were his two favourite foods.

He was a noble animal and he'd nearly talk to you. There was a man called Bill Feeney, who used to work with him on occasions. Bill would sit down and chat with him. He'd chat away as if he was a man. Timmy would be there with the two ears pointed at Bill and he'd be waggling the ears at him.

Timmy obviously knew that Bill was a gentle type of man, so he'd talk to him. People might see the two of them and wonder, 'What the hell! Has Bill gone cracked, talking to a horse?' But Bill would say, 'That horse can talk to you!' He might have been right. He really loved having anything to do with Timmy.

My Uncle Dick had some land that he would let to a couple of guys who set beet, including Bill Feeney. The land was a good long way from us. They'd want to get it ploughed and harrowed. They'd be up looking for Timmy, who was around 30 at that stage. He'd set the beet for them.

You'd have good, long evenings at that time of the year, and when they'd be finished with Timmy around seven or eight o'clock they'd leave him off in the boreen. From there on, he'd be on his own. Up he'd come along the boreen, up the road, over the military road and up to our house where he'd whinny at the gate to let you know he was there. I'd go out and bring him in and take the gear off him. He'd know his own way home.

I would often go for a ride on him when I was a young fellow. I would go bareback and he wouldn't mind in the least. We would go up around the roads, up the hills and back down again. He loved it. The two ears would go up straightaway and you'd see him fully alert. You could see he was back doing what he was used to doing.

He'd be looking for a dog to follow. In particular, if he saw a beagle he'd be really excited and he'd want to go after it. If the hunt was on around the place, he'd want to join that. If he was alone in a field, there would be no bother in him jumping over a ditch and taking off after the hunt. He did it a few times, but he'd come back eventually.

I look back at Timmy very fondly. He must have been in his late 30s when he died. We'd have had other horses, as well, but he was an exception. Other animals could do you in. Some of them would have minds of their own in a different way. They could blow you out of it. I had one animal here, a mare, but you'd want to keep at least six feet away from her back end and at least two feet away from her head. She'd either nail you with a kick or a bite.

You always have to remember with horses that there is a half-a-ton of power there. It just depends on how they use it. But you'd never get that with Timmy. He was laid-back and had a grand easy way about him. He'd never rush and was right casual. For a hunter, he was an extraordinary animal. He was terribly clever and you'd swear he could talk. I've had maybe 30 or 35 horses since him, but Timmy would stand out. I'll never forget him.

**JONATHAN tells about his grandmother's dog, Nero, who helped run the family farm back in the 1940s.**

My granny lived on an isolated farm near Headford in County Galway. She worked the farm with her brother Peadar, having taken it over from my great-grandparents in the 1940s. The farm had lots of different plots of land where they kept cattle and sheep. The two of them had to run the place after my great-grandmother had a stroke.

It was tough on my granny. The house was a little thatched cottage, located down a big boreen, many miles away from the nearest town and with only a few other cottages nearby. It was hard for her to go anywhere. Although Peadar drove a black Morris Minor, all Granny had was a little bike with a basket attached to it. Sometimes, a travelling shop would come to the cottages delivering bread and stuff like that. My granny was very lonely.

It was very quiet in the cottage. The atmosphere was such that you could go for hours without anybody even speaking. It wouldn't be uncommon for everybody to be sitting in silence in the kitchen. It was a real big thing if anybody came up to the house. They would be delighted when visitors arrived and they would be treated very well. The dog would be barking as the visitors drove up the boreen.

Granny could have gone on to college. She had always been a great scholar and good in school. But she had a sister named Nancy and, at that time, there was so much work to be done on the farm that only one of them could avail of a third-level education. It was Nancy who went off to study in Limerick, where she became a shorthand typist.

I think my granny envied Nancy a bit because she used to come home at the weekends with her books and wearing lovely jumpers. Granny would wonder, 'Why couldn't it be me? Why do I have to work on the farm?' She used to cry at night. But she had to stay because Peadar couldn't do everything on his own. They were tough times.

The two of them worked the farm together, along with a dog. Peadar would do the manual work out in the fields, while Granny would look after the chickens. She also worked around the house. The dog – a sheepdog named Nero – worked hard, too. He was black and white, with a white spot over his eye, and he was very good at rounding up sheep. The sheep always listened to him and obeyed him. He was also a great guard dog.

Nero had other skills, as well. For example, when Peadar would be working down in the fields, he would send Nero up to the house to collect something that he needed. He might tell the dog to bring him his pipe or cigarettes. Nero would run straight to the house, which might be miles away. If he was bringing back a packet of cigarettes, there wouldn't be a toothmark on it or the plastic wouldn't be disturbed – he would be that gentle bringing it down in his mouth.

My granny also told me how she would put a bag around his neck and put sandwiches or a flask of tea into it. She might put a note in with the latest news. It might say something like, 'Just to let you know that a man was here asking about the cattle and sheep.' Nero would then dash off down to Peadar. This was before mobile phones and they were communicating back and forth through Nero.

He even carried tools and hammers and screwdrivers down to Peadar. He'd carry them in the bag around his neck. He was also clever enough to avoid places along the way where people might take whatever he was carrying off him. I know there were children living nearby who might have done that. But he'd deliberately avoid them and know the safest way to go, taking back routes, cutting through gaps in walls and heading across fields for safety. He was a really clever dog.

He also used to eat with them in the kitchen, where they had a range and a table. He would sit down on the kitchen floor when they sat down at the table. If they had potatoes and meat, he would have that, too. He always had the same food as they had. When they would have tea, he would have tea from his own cup on the floor. He also slept under Peadar's bed, in his own place. He was like part of the family.

Nero eventually died from old age. One day, they had his dinner laid out but he wasn't there. They went looking for him and started calling him. They eventually found him in the barn, wrapped up in one of Peadar's work jackets. He was already dead. Granny said she was in tears for weeks.

They had another dog after that, called Brandy. He wasn't a patch on Nero. They could never train him to do the things Nero could do. There was only one thing he mastered – he could get a packet of biscuits out of the press and carry the packet over to them. Otherwise, compared to Nero, he was only second-rate, in the halfpenny place.

When I was young, I would go up and visit the cottage and I'd hear all about Nero. Even today, my granny still talks about him. That's 60 or 70 years later and she speaks about him as much as ever. If anybody brings up a story about a dog, she goes, 'I remember when Peadar and I used to have a dog named Nero.' Then she describes what he did. She really loved him.

As a result, I've always loved animals and our family has kept dogs ever since. The love of them has passed down through the family. I think they are so smart. They pick up on what's going on. They can do so many things. Our dog is like that, and he is treated like a prince at home.

From what I hear, though, it would be hard to match Nero. My granny always believed that sheepdogs are the most intelligent dogs that you can get. She would swear by them and loved their friendly manner. But Nero seems to have been an exceptional dog, really smart, a worker, a runner and a living mobile phone – he did it all.

ÁINE KEANE **outlines how a dog named Louis has been an enormous support to her autistic son Brian.**

My second child, Brian, was born in September 2008, during the month when the economy collapsed. I knew from day one that there was something different about him. He was a very difficult baby, very hard to settle. The nurse was saying, 'You've had a girl, so far, and you can't compare a girl to a boy. Boys are always much crosser babies. They don't hit their milestones as quickly.' But I had a mother's instinct that something was wrong.

The following year, I was still pushing to get something done with Brian. He was still very difficult, not sleeping and was horrendously cross. That year, when he was 12 months old and I was turning 40, I decided I would treat myself to a dog. I wanted a giant dog but one suitable to children. A vet said, 'Have you ever heard of Leonbergers?' I hadn't.

I looked them up and they are very rare. They are known for their placid nature and they are very big. They are hard to get, but I eventually got one. He was born in September 2009. He is like a lion, very hairy, with a reddish-gold colour and a dark face. We were trying to think of a name. We were watching *The X Factor* and we saw Louis Walsh. He reminded us of him, so we called him Louis.

I had already noticed with Brian that his eye contact with us was very poor and he hated affection. Normally, if a baby is upset, you console them by hugging them or kissing them, but Brian couldn't bear that. All we could do was put him into a rocking chair and let him rock and the motion would soothe him. We discovered, though, that he was making good contact with Louis and he was very affectionate with him. But we still didn't know something was wrong.

We finally got a formal diagnosis of autism when Brian was about two and a half. When he was about four, he started in a special preschool and he made huge progress from four to six. He went from being non-verbal to fully verbal. He also went from not being toilet-trained to being fully toilet-trained. He ended up in mainstream school, as well, which was great.

All that time, and right up to the present day, he has had a real bond with Louis. When we go out walking now, Brian will take the lead and walk Louis. That's not easy as Louis is really disobedient and we often say he suffers from selective deafness. He does things when he's ready, not when you're ready. I actually took him to the vet because I thought he might be partially deaf. But Louis, who is about nine stone, will obey Brian.

Louis lies down a lot and chills out. If Brian lies on top of him or manhandles him, it's not a problem. If Louis is lying in the sitting-room and Brian decides he wants to give him a cuddle, he might lie on top of him. Louis is fine with that and will give Brian a lick in the face. He never gets cranky with Brian.

When Brian gets up in the morning, he always goes to the kitchen and he says good morning to Louis. Mind you, Louis might only lift the head as he is not much of a morning person! When Brian calls Louis, he always comes to him; he will only sometimes do that with me. Most of all, though, Louis is a calming influence. Brian will sit quietly and is always in a good mood when he's around Louis.

The two of them can be trouble, too. I remember, especially when they were young, every time I heard a crash or a noise I thought it must be one of them who was the cause. I actually started to call them Double Trouble or The Terrible Twosome. It got to the stage where I could confuse their names – I'd find myself saying 'Brian' when it would be Louis I'd be talking to and 'Louis' when I'd be talking to Brian. They were a right pair!

We later found out that Leonbergers are great with autistic children. We discovered that Louis's dad is a qualified therapy dog and he goes to a centre for autistic children. We also found out that another family has one of Louis's younger siblings and their child has severe autism. That family found that since they got their dog it has made a big difference. It seems it's in the breeding.

Getting him was like fate at work. I picked Louis because I liked the look of him and thought he would be a good family dog. But I didn't know that Brian would be diagnosed with autism and I certainly didn't think that Louis would work out the way he did. I often wonder if we hadn't got Louis would Brian have made all the progress he did make.

Today, Brian is doing very well and is more or less on a par with his peers. He's fully verbal. If you met him, you mightn't realise he has autism – 99 per cent of the time it's not apparent. I am thrilled with that. At the age of four, we certainly didn't think he would have made this progress. The first contact he made was with Louis and he still shows affection to him. I think we were very lucky to have found that dog.

**ANNA MAY GALLAGHER recalls two of her favourite collies who worked on the family farm.**

The first one I had was pure white, with a black spot above her tail and a wee black spot on her face. I bought her as a pup on the day that Donegal won the All-Ireland in 1992. She was about six months old, with long ears and a great coat of hair. She was a real pet and as crafty as anything.

The person that I got her from called her Spot. However, my mother had an uncle whose name was Ned, or Edward. For whatever reason, he ended up being called Dot. I really have no idea why. So, when I got Spot, I decided to call her Dot. That's what she was called to the day she died.

She was a great sheepdog. She would go up to the top of a mountain and bring the sheep down to you for dipping, clipping or dosing. We had maybe 400 sheep at the time. I would say, 'Go away up for the sheep, Dot!' She could go! She would fly up and help bring them down bit by bit. She would also go after the ten or 12 that might be far up the mountain on their own and bring them down. She got plenty of exercise alongside the other dogs we had at that stage.

Dot was never aggressive unless the sheep didn't move for her. Sometimes, one or two of them might face her up. She might give them a wee nip and that would make them go. When she'd get them down, she would know she had done it. I would say, 'Very good dog, Dot!' and that would make her feel twice as good.

She sensed when people were fond of her. There were two people living nearby. When one of them would be going down the lane, she would walk on the other side and turn her head away from him; she would never glance at him except maybe occasionally to give him a sarcastic look. When the other would walk by, she would be all pals with him. Sheepdogs can be like that. They get notions.

Do you want to know what I did one day? We had been marking up the sheep with blue and red. I thought, 'I'll do Dot up!' She was pure white, but I made up her cheeks with red and I put blue around her eyes, like eye shadow. I brought her down the road to collect some sheep and a young lad looked at the dog and he nearly collapsed. My husband wasn't amused. Later on, I thought of doing her up in the Donegal colours but I changed my mind.

Dot was 11 years of age when she died. About six months later, in 2003, we got Jip. She was so crafty! She was very brainy and would know what you were thinking. Everyone who saw her thought she was the nicest dog. She loved ice cream and she was a great friend of mine. She was very sensitive and would know if I was in bad humour. She understood every word I was saying.

She was good at rounding up sheep, too, but she was choosy about who she would work for. She would often only work for me and refuse to work for my husband. Sheepdogs can be like that. If you didn't talk nice to her, or be nice to her, she'd let you sit there. She had her own personality and her own way of doing things. She wouldn't do all the things everybody would want her to do, but she would do them for me.

Jip was always ready for the road. Every time I started to prepare to go out, she was heading for the jeep and ready to jump in. If I only started to wash my face, she would know. Once the water ran outside from the bathroom, she was on her way. But when Sunday morning came, she never rose out of her bed. We'd be going to Mass, but she never moved. It's funny what they know!

Jip was also very protective. I could go to Dublin and leave my jeep sitting in the middle of the street and it would never be robbed. She would never let anybody next or near it. She would be sitting on the front passenger seat and people might come over to look in the window. The window on her side of the jeep would be all scraped from her claws. She'd be trying to keep the people away from the jeep.

She was also protective of me on the day she won a rosette in a dog show. She was bossing all the other dogs that were there. She thought she was saving me and making sure I was OK. Even when people came by to the window of the jeep, I couldn't open it because she was trying to protect me. When people would try to sit into the jeep, she'd be the same.

Jip was around ten or 11 when she died and I have had more sheepdogs since. I have three of them now, but Dot and Jip were my two favourites. They mightn't have been as good at working as other dogs, but they were two genuine pets. All collies are beautiful dogs to own, very clean and friendly, the nicest dogs you will see. They are lovely dogs. But of all of them, Dot and Jip are the two I will always remember.

**PADDY DOYLE speaks about the very special dog in the life of his brother, the legendary Tipperary hurler Jimmy Doyle.**

Jimmy was always very fond of dogs, but Billy was his favourite. He was a really adorable dog, a small black-and-white collie. Whenever Jimmy went up to the outside field at Semple Stadium, he'd go there with the dog. In the summer he'd have all the other players from Thurles Sarsfields there, but in winter he would only have Billy.

In the afternoon or early evening, he'd go up to the field and bring Billy with him along with a bag of balls. Jimmy would take frees. The balls would either go over the bar or wide, and the dog would run after them and bring them back to his feet. Jimmy wouldn't just hit one and wait for Billy to bring it back. Instead, he would hit five or six and Billy would know where all the balls were. He'd bring all of them back every time. He never lost a ball.

Jimmy also told me that every time he'd raise a ball to hit it, Billy would jump and try to snap it with his mouth while it was in the air. As a result, Jimmy developed a technique where, as he lifted the ball to hit it, he'd bring it back in towards him. He told me many times that that technique developed from Billy trying to snap the ball from him.

Jimmy would also insist on hitting ten points in a row. He wouldn't leave the field until he had done that. They were never easy frees. He would insist on going from one side of the field to the other. If Jimmy hit a wide after nine frees, he'd start all over again.

No matter how late it got, he'd have to get the ten in a row. As a result, my mother used to have trouble with him; she'd come to the gate looking for him as it got dark. Billy would stay with him the whole time, bringing all the balls back. Then the two of them would come home together.

Jimmy really adored that dog and the dog adored Jimmy. In the morning, Jimmy would come down for breakfast and Billy would meet him at the end of the stairs. He'd be wagging his tail, thinking he'd be going up to the hurling field. When Jimmy would come home to the house, Billy would be waiting for him at the door and would greet him. He would often have a ball in his mouth, like he was telling him, 'I'm ready, if you're ready, to go up to the field!'

Billy would even go down with Jimmy to the CBS, where we went to school. He wouldn't go with me, only Jimmy. When Jimmy would go into school, he'd stay at the gate. When Jimmy would come out, he'd be waiting for him at the gate. He'd do that every day knowing he would then be going up to the field. When Jimmy would produce the bag of balls, Billy would be jumping all over the place.

Jimmy and Billy were together for four or five years from the mid-1950s to the later 1950s. Jimmy eventually won six senior and three minor All-Irelands, along with seven league medals. He was also voted onto the Team of the Century and Team of the Millennium. I really believe that Billy had a big role to play in those achievements, especially in terms of Jimmy's skills. Jimmy did so many things on his own, but he always said that Billy had a lot to do with the development of his hurling.

It was just like a death in the family when Billy died. We all adored him; everyone on the street adored him, too. He was such a gentle and beautiful dog. Jimmy was brokenhearted. You can imagine how it affected him, especially given how affectionate he was towards Billy and how loyal Billy was in return. All of a sudden, Billy was gone. It was so sad.

Jimmy died in June 2015. He had always loved his dogs, not cats, just dogs, and he especially loved Billy. His happiest days were when he was a minor, around the time of Billy. It was real affection, and he was a beautiful dog. He had dogs later on, but nothing compared to the original Billy. Up to the day he died, Jimmy spoke with huge affection about him. He absolutely adored him, without a doubt.

**In the mid-1950s, ROSALEEN grew up on a farm where her dog Rover was her closest companion and best friend.**

Rover was a sheepdog, kind of sandy-coloured. His hair was down on his face and you could hardly see his eyes. It was as if he didn't want people to identify him or to know who he was or where he had come from. I liked that. There was a bit of a mystery about him.

We lived a life of solitude in the country. Rover knew that I wasn't allowed to go dancing or to the carnival, or anything like that. All I was told to do was kneel down and pray for forgiveness or whatever I was supposed to pray for. He would sit beside me on the concrete floor, with his head down, while I prayed. He would never do that with the others, only me.

I would talk to Rover and sing to him. He would put his head up in the air and make noises as if he was copying me. Of course, I can't sing at all, but I thought I was great. I'd be sitting there like a fool, singing away with the dog. If I wasn't in the mood to sing to him or to talk to him, he just sat with his head straight down on the floor. He always picked up the mood of the moment and knew how I was feeling. He was a very sensitive dog.

Rover was very close to me. At times, when the fire would go out, Rover would come with me to get some wood. I'd break branches off the trees in the fields. I remember there would be moss in a river that I had to cross. I'd slip on the moss and the branches would all fall in the river. He'd be there to pick the sticks up with his mouth. He'd always be at my side.

He even came along with me to school. I had to walk the three or four miles to get there. He would be beside me. We would pass farmhouses where there would be trained guard dogs. If I were on my own, they would chase me and bark viciously. But with Rover there, that didn't happen. The time came when not one dog would come out and challenge me.

He was allowed to sit with me at school. The teacher said, 'You can have the dog in class, but he's got to sit down.' I had trained him to do that, so he sat down and was as good as gold. On one occasion, however, the teacher decided to cane me for something to do with geography, I think. The minute he went to strike my hand, Rover went for him and grabbed him by the sleeve.

The teacher said, 'Right! Your dog goes home! Get him out of here immediately!' I took Rover out and set him in the direction of home. I said, 'Go! Rover! Go!' My mother later said he arrived looking like he had run without stopping. His heart was going so fast. He was wet, as well. He was worried from then on that I was in danger at school.

One day, he took a real dislike to the postman. He had been going along on his bike. He had letters for my mother. He rolled them up and was trying to put them into Rover's mouth so that he would carry them. I said, 'Don't do that or the dog will bite you!' He said, 'He's only a cat. He wouldn't touch anyone.'

Well, the dog took him by the trousers and tore the whole leg off down to his ankle. The postman had to go in to my mother and she stitched his trousers together again. She did it with him standing up. The postman never tried that trick again!

On the other hand, he never touched a pigeon that came to stay with us at the farm. He had broken his wing and I fixed it with some matches and string. I got the wing back in place again. That pigeon wouldn't go away. It stayed for four years. I would take him out into the garden and let him fly. He would just fly in a circle and come down at my feet again. But Rover never attacked him; they got on really well.

Rover was really protective. My father would go off walking in the fields with the dog. He suffered from angina. Sometimes, he would collapse on the banks of the river nearby. The dog would come home looking for me. He would keep barking and looking up at me, making it clear that he wanted me to follow him. He'd lead me to where my dad was and I'd get him up on his feet and home.

One day, the dog came back home without my father but he wouldn't take me anywhere. He kept walking around normally. I panicked. I wondered, 'What's going on?' I thought, 'The dog knows more than he's telling me. Maybe something bad has happened to my dad and he has died.'

Eventually, the dog did take me to my dad. The funny thing was that it was the last time my dad got an angina attack. The dog must have known that my dad was on the way to a good recovery. He felt, 'There's no point in my looking anxious anymore because it's not necessary.'

As I got older, I went to Dublin and trained to be a nanny. I soon heard that Rover had gone blind. Then I heard that a car had hit him and he had been killed on the road. I was devastated. It was like telling me that everyone in the nearest town had died. There had been Rover, my father and I. We had a great bond. And now Rover was gone.

I don't know what I'd have done without him, to tell you the truth. He was really more than a dog. He wasn't just like any dog; he was a dog like no other. There were loads of dogs around, but none like him. He was an absolute miracle. I feel maybe God had given him to me because somebody had to be on my side. He became part of my life, my friend when I was on my own. I truly believe that he was sent.

**CORMAC WILLIAMS has eight donkeys on his family farm in County Kerry. Although donkeys were once used for work purposes on the farm, they are now treated as pets and entertain farm-holiday guests.**

In the main, donkeys are clever. I can tell you a very interesting story. There is a man in Milltown, on the west side of Killarney, who had a donkey and a very nice garden. The garden was really well-managed. He had this gridding system in the ground at the entry to the garden to stop animals from going in.

Despite the grid, he used to find that a donkey was getting into the garden. After a while, he began thinking that someone must have been doing it on purpose. He thought it could only have been happening if the donkey was being put in over the grid. Someone must have been doing it to get on his nerves.

It eventually transpired that the donkey discovered that he couldn't step over the grid so he used to lie down and roll over it. He had it figured out what to do. He knew that if he stepped on the grid, his hoofs would have gone in. Donkeys like to roll and they do it a lot, and he had decided to use this ability and to roll into the garden.

He was also clever enough, when it came to getting him out, not to let on how he did it and roll back out again. He wasn't going to facilitate the guy with the lawn and let him know. If he had been there for long enough and got tired of the garden, he would probably have started to roll, but you couldn't force a donkey to do it. The donkey would decide himself when to do the rolling.

Growing up during the 1960s, we always had donkeys. They were used on the farm for little jobs. Given their size, they were suitable only for smaller jobs. They would take milk to the creamery, bring little loads out to the fields, and transport things around the farm.

Tractors didn't really come in until the late 1960s in Kerry, and up to a few years before that around 90 per cent of people would have had horses or donkeys for farming. Down here, they would pull little carts and not carry the baskets which would be used for bogs in the West of Ireland. Like many other people, I would have taken milk to the creamery using a donkey.

I have eight donkeys now, but my main one is Bessy. She is a traditional brown donkey with the cross on her back. She is very placid, gentle and genteel. She wouldn't have the giddiness of ponies or the nervousness of horses. When I go out to the field, she'll come up to me and rub herself against me. She loves the petting and the attention.

I have Bessy about 30 years, but donkeys can live to about 40, especially nowadays when they are well-treated and do less work. She might not have the verbalisation of a cat or a dog, by purring or yelping, but she can express herself through her big open eyes. I'm sure she has the thought at the back of her mind that she is capable of getting some reward from you, like an apple.

Bessy, like all donkeys, can be stubborn, although she tends to be much more placid than most. If you try to take a donkey somewhere they don't want to go, you are up against it. They go into reverse gear. They pull backwards against you. It's their defence mechanism. I don't know why they do it. They must have brought the trait with them from North Africa, where they originally came from.

There is a wandering streak in them, as well. If you leave a gate open, they will try to get out. Even if they are a distance from the gate, they will head off. They have an innate instinct to do that, even though they are going nowhere. They would just wander the road or go to the next paddock. They would watch the gate and look for an opening to escape through and move on.

They love carrots and apples, but they are not interested in good grass. They don't eat lush grass like horses would. They tend to go along a fence and eat weeds. They eat rushes and briars, especially in winter. They like rough fodder and are more of a foraging animal. It's something within them that tells them to go for a rougher diet. It must be something they brought with them.

They also can bite. I remember, one day, we were doing some photos with kids and they had some carrots. I took the bit out of Bessy's mouth and I was talking to a child while breaking up her carrots. Bessy caught my finger. I can tell you I got a fine nip. When you get a nip from a donkey's teeth, by God you can feel it. But Bessy didn't mean it. They really don't bite like ponies and horses.

They will rarely kick, but they are certainly able to do so. Sometimes, when I'd be with the donkeys, I might have my dog with me and she might be messing around. She might be a bit jealous of the attention I'm giving them and maybe catch one of them by the hind foot. I've often seen them kicking back and connecting. Again, it's a defensive thing. I wouldn't like to get the full force of it.

Bessy has foaled around 12 or 15 times. An interesting thing about her, like all donkeys, is that about 99.9 per cent of them will foal at night. If labour is coming on, they can hold it back until night arrives. I've never known them to foal by day. It's an amazing thing. That, again, must come from way back.

Bessy is the grandmother of twins. Her daughter was Tulip and she, in turn, had twins named Snow and Flake. We called them that because it was late November when they were born, just before Christmas, and there was snow on the hilltops here in Kerry. They were beautiful donkeys, very white with a bit of speckling.

It wasn't rare to have twins, but it was rare that they both lived. In the event of twins, one or two of them will be born dead. I was looking, at the time, to give them to a live crib but unfortunately they didn't have a live crib in Killarney that year. They could have had the mother, as well, because the twins were young at the time and they wouldn't have been weaned.

In the 1980s, I opened a self-catering holiday home on the farm here in Brewsterfield and I use Bessy for cart rides for kids. She gives them little rides around the farm. The kids love her. Donkeys are a huge novelty to them. You can imagine why. You just don't see them in cities like Berlin, Paris or London. So it's gone full circle for me. What was used for the farm in the 1960s is now used for the tourist industry.

Just like the visitors, I also really like donkeys. They are very placid and genteel and affectionate, much more so than horses or ponies who are more standoffish and temperamental. They are so lovable, so good-natured, and they are beautiful animals. They like affection and they will return it far more readily than ponies or horses. I think they are wonderful creatures, really lovely, the friendliest animals you will ever meet.

**CLAIRE HENNESSY describes how the acquisition of a beautiful Labrador Retriever changed her children's perception of dogs. The dog also developed a close bond with her son Patrick, who is blind.**

Our three children were terrified of dogs. When I'd drive into somebody's driveway, they would crunch their legs underneath them in case a dog was going to take their legs off! I would have to ask the owners to put away the dog or ask them if the dog would bite. All three children were equally bad. It was absolutely disastrous.

Apart from the other two being scared of dogs, I have a son Patrick who is totally blind. His eyes didn't develop. He goes to mainstream school and he is doing famously, but I thought maybe down the line Patrick might need a dog. I wondered if we needed to change our attitude to them.

I was against having a dog in the house. I had been brought up with farm dogs but not with having an animal with four legs going around the house. About five years ago, however, when Patrick was eight, my husband Pat and I began to think that having a dog might be a good decision long-term. It might help deal with the fear of dogs, if nothing else.

We got on to the guide dog centre just to have a look. Some of the dogs they train work out as guide dogs, but others don't. They thought of getting us a companion who had failed as a guide dog but who was going to have to be rehomed. It suited us, as we were looking for an animal that was friendly. Patrick was too young, anyway, to qualify for a guide dog.

Everyone else who was visiting was looking at these lovely little puppies, but not my lot. The screaming and roaring out of the three of them was beyond belief! At one stage, I ended up saying, 'Will you shut up. We're never going to get a dog at this rate.' We eventually filled in the relevant forms and were told they had a dog for us if we were interested.

Hogan arrived and he was absolutely beautiful, a nice golden colour and young. Labrador Retrievers are so friendly towards children and we were assured there was going to be no biting or anything like that. That's exactly how it turned out – he was disciplined and would never snap or attack anyone.

Ruby, our youngest, who was really terrified of dogs, spent the first week on the kitchen table. I had to carry her from room to room in case she would lose a leg! She laughs at that now. Michaela, who was the eldest, was OK, and Patrick loved him from the start.

Very quickly, it was clear that he was ours forever. He arrived with a bell, which he doesn't have now. It was great having it as Patrick could hear the dog jingling along. By now, Patrick's senses are so heightened that he knows where the dog is anyway, but the bell was handy at the time.

Patrick can now sense when Hogan is present. He might know it from sound. He sometimes uses echolocation. For example, if he's coming to a door you will notice he walks a little slower because he knows there's a wall nearby. He can use it to sense Hogan, as well.

From the start, Patrick and Hogan got on really well. Patrick would hang around him. He would be rubbing Hogan's fur or lying beside him. He loved to lie along with Hogan in the bed which the dog had under the stairs. There was a calmness and warmth about Hogan that he liked.

Patrick might be having his tea or he might be in the kitchen doing something and Hogan would be around. It was just like having another person there. Patrick might sometimes want to listen to an audio book and not want people present because he'll want peace and quiet to listen to it, but Hogan will be there and not intruding.

It is also great to have the dog with Patrick when he is in the house on his own. We might be nervous that someone would come knocking on the front door, yet we have to allow Patrick independence especially now that he is 13. If I have to go out for some reason, there's a bit of security in the dog being in the house.

The other two children adapted very quickly to Hogan, too. Within a short couple of weeks, Ruby would crawl along under Hogan. The fear was gone. She developed a relationship with him that has lasted over time. They all got over their fear and they are not as bad with other dogs, either. Patrick will even sit with my brother's dogs and he is very content.

The only thing Hogan doesn't like is when the children play the concertina. He moans and he groans and he cries. He really doesn't like it. All three play instruments. Michaela plays the concertina and does drama and sings a bit. Ruby plays the concertina and is an Irish dancer, as well. Patrick plays piano and the drums. But Hogan certainly hates the concertina.

Despite that, they like Hogan so much that one day they rebelled against me. I was desperately late to my mother's house with a cooked chicken. I couldn't be late. It had to arrive at a certain time. We were travelling along, with Hogan down on the floor by the passenger seat. Someone must have spilled something and I stopped to get some wipes.

I opened the door and Hogan got out. I could not get him back into the car. Here we were, two miles from our house, and I said, 'You know what, Hogan? You can stay there!' You should have heard the children. They went ballistic. They were roaring, in convulsions.

I didn't want a dog, yet now I find myself talking to Hogan. He is like another person in the house. We all now know the real Hogan. He is so calm and sedate. If someone arrives at the house, he'll get all excited and flustered but once they're gone he becomes his calm self again.

Hogan is Hogan and he just floats around. He is now quite lazy, especially since some of the training has worn off. But I am so glad we got him. If we hadn't, all three children would still have a fear of dogs; it might even have got worse. So I am absolutely thrilled for the three of them, including Patrick who now talks of getting a guide dog when he's older. Hogan has changed everything for them for the rest of their lives.

PAULA DORRINGTON **talks about her extraordinary guide dog Zane, who she got from Irish Guide Dogs for the Blind.**

I have the first guide dog that has been trained to tell low blood sugar. He does it by scent. I have a little kit that tells what my blood sugar is. If Zane thinks the blood sugar is very low, or that I'm not responsive enough to him, he'll put his head on my lap and then he'll go and get the kit off the table and bring it over and put it on my lap. He'll keep banging it on my lap until I test the blood sugar for him.

If I don't respond quick enough, he will go to my husband and keep going from him back to me and back again until something is done. My husband will eventually say, 'Paula, I think you had better test your blood sugar. Zane is doing a lot of moving around.' After I do the test, I will give him a treat and he then goes straight over to his mat and sits down. It's like he says, 'OK, it's all over now! That's grand! I've done that!' He is absolutely incredible.

If I am out with him and he's on harness and he senses my blood sugar is low, he knows he has to behave himself so much better, so he will do things differently. He will just stand there with his head on my lap and put his paw up. He doesn't do all the moving around that he will do with me at home. He does it quietly, as if to say, 'I know you're going to get the kit out now, in a minute, but if you don't I will stand on you and put my two paws up on you.'

Zane is a Golden Retriever and I got him about three years ago, when he was a year and a half. I had three guide dogs before him. I have had no sight at all for about the last 25 years. I'm blind from diabetes, which I have had since I was nine. My husband Gus has ten per cent sight in one eye. He works all day and I'm in the house on my own from seven in the morning until five in the evening.

I have had a problem with low blood sugar for ten years, or more, and I've landed up in hospital in comas. It's linked to the diabetes. But now that I have Zane, this is one of the longest spells where I haven't had people giving me injections to get me out of a low blood sugar problem. I have Zane to thank for that.

Zane is also a guide dog for me. I couldn't move out of the house without him. I wouldn't be able to go shopping every day. I couldn't go horse riding, which I do now. I couldn't even get from the front door to the gate without Zane. In the house, he walks around with me from room to room, but he's not necessary there. Otherwise, he's essential.

We might go out with him to the shops or to coffee shops or to a bus stop. The trips would involve crossing a major road. I would instruct him which way to go. I might say, 'Keep going! Straight on!' Once I say that, he knows that we're probably going for lunch. If I say, 'Right, Zane!' he knows we're going to the shops and not going for lunch just yet. Coming back, if I don't tell him to go straight on he'll turn slightly left and he'll head to the shops.

So it's really a mixture of verbal commands along with intuitive understanding. It's very important to get that combination right because Zane is so clever that he will try to decide for himself where we're going. He will mostly decide the right place, but you might want to go somewhere else. It's important to tell him well in advance what we're going to do and how we're going to do it.

Another feature of Zane is that he walks exactly by my side. He is never a step ahead of me. He puts his two front paws up on a step and stands there and waits until I put my first foot up on the step. Then, when I get my second foot up on the step, he brings his back paws up. He is extraordinary doing that.

He is so content and so good. He's not distracted by other dogs or by people coming up to him. People coming to pet him can be a problem, especially because he is such a good-looking dog. I will say, 'Sorry, he's working at the moment.' But I do notice that, although they pet him, he doesn't pay any attention.

It can also happen in a coffee shop. I will always know when someone is looking at him because he starts wagging the tail. I know what's happening around me because Zane's tail wags. Otherwise, he sits there and never moves and the head always stays down. I will mostly explain to people who come up to pet him that he is a guide dog. It's always good for people to understand what a guide dog is about.

Zane can be great fun, too. Although I can't see him, people tell me he lies down and rolls over. He also has a free run when I go horse riding. He's off the harness and lead. But he doesn't like to see me going cantering. If he cannot keep up with the horse, he starts to bark. He's afraid I'm going away from him. That seems to frighten him a little. He also has fun playing ball with my husband. He has a blanket he plays with and he loves having his belly rubbed.

He has also come skiing with us to Austria. People loved him on the slopes. He used to run ahead of us and wait at one of the coffee places where we would stop. He'd get there before us and the people loved him. The owners of the place couldn't get enough of him. He wasn't useful from a skiing point of view, but he was invaluable around the village. Once he saw our hotel room the first time, he could find it again from then on.

It's amazing how bright he is. We were in Arnotts department store one day and he suddenly went over to this woman. She said to me, 'That's not Zane, is it?' I said, 'Yes.' She said, 'I'm the sister of the lady who puppy-trained him.' She had recognised him and Zane had recognised her. He put out the paw to her. We couldn't believe it. She couldn't believe it, either.

Do I like him? I love him. He is so good. He means an awful lot to me and I think I mean an awful lot to him. We don't have any children, but he is like a child to us. We would do anything for him. He is my eyesight. He is essential to me.

His intelligence is second to none. He is brilliantly trained. A guide dog lasts for ten years, but what Zane does regarding low blood sugar lasts forever. So, as far as I'm concerned, Zane will never retire from me. There's 24 hours in a day and he's with me all 24 hours. He's essential to me, and long may our relationship last.

**JOHN MC GRATH explains how he and his wife Olive came to host a Labrador puppy which needed training as a guide dog for the blind. The dog was named Jody.**

I saw on the back of a newspaper, one day, that there was a Labrador who had 12 puppies and the people from Irish Guide Dogs for the Blind were looking for the puppies to be trained. They sent two people down to investigate whether our place would be suitable or not. They warned my wife Olive that the dog would dig up the plants and would be very active in its younger days. She said, 'We'll get over that.'

They said our place would be suitable and we were approved for a dog. They told us they'd bring down a medical card and all the paraphernalia that went with her. Down they arrived with the puppy, a bed, a blanket, a bone, a whistle, a guide dog booklet to tell us how to train her, and a lead. They also brought us a fireguard.

I said, 'I can understand all of those things except for the fireguard. What's that for?' They told us that what we should do was put the dog's bed in the corner, put the puppy into the bed, put the fireguard in front of the bed, and place a few newspapers between the fireguard and the bed. The dog could only go as far as the fireguard during the night, so she would go to the toilet on the papers.

They informed us that in the morning we should pick up the puppy, pick up the papers, bring the dog out to the yard and say, 'Busy! Busy!' That's what we did. Would you believe it, within a week that dog was toilet-trained! When we went out to the yard, she would do her pee and never messed in the house again. Strange to say, that fireguard was a critical part of the training.

We got the dog, Jody, for a year. They were very particular about what we should do. We couldn't allow the dog up on the couch; under no circumstances was that permissible. When we took her on the beach, we had to bring a biscuit with us. You'd let the dog off on the beach and you'd use the whistle to call her back. You'd reward her for coming back by giving her some biscuit.

One of the things that I wondered about was how to stop the dog from rambling away from me. I took her out to a part of the beach which also contained sand dunes. I'd leave the dog on the beach and run up onto the dunes and wait until she'd start worrying and looking for me. Eventually, I'd let her find me. After that, I noticed that the dog would stay close to me. She started going ahead of me by a few yards and looking behind to see was I still there.

It was a great experience to go through all the training. At the end of the year, they came and said, 'It's time to take away the dog.' At that stage, the dog was house-trained and basically ready. What it needed after that was to be taken into shops and onto buses and things like that. I was sad to see her go because I had loved it. Olive, who had put in huge work, was also sad to see her go. I suppose there's something between a human and an animal – they can show such affection for each other.

When the dog was about two years old, I remember getting a call from Dublin. This lady said, 'I'd like to meet you.' She told me that she was completely blind and had got the dog I had trained. She came down and we met in a local hotel. Olive and I went to meet her. What happened was most interesting. She told us some amazing stories about the dog, but she also wondered would the dog know me.

The dog had been sitting under the table. I put my hand in and she wagged her tail, but I really wasn't sure that she had recognised me. The lady said, 'Jody needs to relieve herself. Why don't you take her to the nearby park?' Jody wouldn't leave. I had to give her a good few tugs before she'd go with me. And off to the park we went.

Amazingly, we struck up an immediate relationship again. We went around the park, she did her business, and I picked it up and disposed of it. We had a lovely time together. Maybe about 15 or 20 minutes passed by and I brought her back. The moment I got there, she went back under the table and there was a cut-off again. It was like, 'Nice to have met you again, John, but this is my master now and this is my job.' It was amazing to see.

The whole meeting was very rewarding. The lady recognised how much effort I had put into training Jody. She knew that the dog was well-trained and she wanted to meet the person responsible, and I was that person. She had travelled 150 miles to meet me. She told us stories about the dog. It was a lovely day and a lovely thing to happen.

I took other dogs after that. I did four or five altogether and, believe me, it was a hugely rewarding thing to do. There was a beautiful black Labrador I had at one stage, who had a gland problem and was rejected. I was offered the dog to keep, but I didn't take him because I knew I wouldn't ever again get to train any other puppies. I really regret not taking him; he was so wonderful.

But nothing could compare to Jody, the first one. She was such a joy. People have asked me how I ever parted with her or, indeed, how I parted with all the others. The truth is that I believed I was doing a service to somebody who was visually impaired. It was so rewarding to know that so many people could function as a result of the work I had put in. In that sense, I thought nothing of it.

**PADDY FINN describes how he and his dog Snoop have looked after each other in illness and in health.**

My daughter got the dog initially, about nine years ago. She only had him a short while when she was affected by the recession. Just as the crisis was starting, she went away to

London. She came back for a couple of months and then went to live in Australia. He was only a little pup when I took him in.

The dog is called Snoop. He's a half King Charles and a half Jack Russell. He's a lovely little thing, the same as a Jack Russell but with the head of a King Charles. He is brown and white and really beautiful. Every time I walk him, people remark on how lovely he is.

He's like a child. He's almost too friendly. He'd lick me all day if he could. He'll sit at my feet when I'm sitting down. He puts his legs out flat and lies there. The minute I move, he will come to me. He'll always lie at the bottom of the stairs if I go out. He'll wait there until I come home. He's really the best friend and best company you could ever have.

I feed him in the morning and at night. When I'm eating, he rubs my leg and I have to feed him more. I always put two extra sausages on for him. I go to the charity shops and get him lovely rugs. I have to tell him, 'These are not for me, they are for you.' He loves them. I give him two treats every night. He's better looked after than I am.

I got diabetes in the late 1990s. I'm also asthmatic and I've had a bypass. I have to check my blood four times a day before I eat. I have to take my injections four times a day, as well. I keep a chart of how many units I take. Snoop is always with me when I'm doing this. He's at my feet, looking after me. He's around me the whole time.

I have always known that if I collapsed, he'd go looking for somebody to help me. Even if it happened at home, he'd scratch the door to get someone in off the road. He's that clever. He always knows what I'm doing and he looks out for me.

One day, I realised that he was drinking more water than I was. That was about three years ago. He was drinking and drinking and drinking, even drinking dirty water. I brought him to the vet. I said, 'I think my dog is diabetic.' He said, 'What makes you think that?' So I told him. He took him in the next morning, did the tests and told me, 'You're right, he's a diabetic.'

The vet told me, 'There are two things you can do. You can either have a hard job for the rest of your life injecting him and looking after him, or you can get him put down.' I said, 'That's like you telling my wife to put me down because I'm a diabetic.'

I felt terrible. I was devastated at the thought of it. Snoop was always really lovely to me. I wouldn't put him down, no way. The dog looked at me as if he knew what was going on. So I told the vet I'd be keeping him. When he heard I was also a diabetic, he said, 'Well, he'll be on the very same injections you are on.' So I started to look after Snoop.

We now both have diabetes. I give him his injections twice a day. He knows they are coming up. He actually turns his head for me to inject him. I keep moving him around so I don't give them to him in just the one place. I check his blood, as well. Otherwise, he could go into a coma.

If he's high, I'll inject him, walk him and then feed him. It's the same for me, except I inject myself four times a day. I treat him the same as myself. I could go into a coma, too. If my blood is high, I take my injection, go for a walk and eat when I come back. We do it all together.

Unfortunately, he became blind as a result of the diabetes. It started about a year after Snoop was diagnosed. I started to notice things; other people did, too. Although he's completely blind now, he still functions well. If I am coming up the road in my car, he will run up after me. Even though he's blind, he knows it's me. He still lives a normal life.

I lost him one time. I looked for him everywhere. I offered a reward in the vet's place and in shops. Eventually, this lady rang me. She said, 'I know where the dog is.' She gave me an address about seven or eight miles away. I went to the place and knocked at the door. I said, 'I believe you found a dog.' The woman denied it. When I said that I would have to tell the guards, she said, 'Yes, I did find one.'

I asked her if I could have a look at him. She brought him out and he ran to me straightaway. He was thrilled. I asked her, 'How did he happen to get out here?' She gave me some daft story about Snoop hopping into her car and she took him with her. Why didn't she put him back out? Anyway, Snoop was delighted to see me and I brought him home again.

I'm 70 years of age now. Snoop is nearly ten, which in human terms is about the same as me. So we're both about the same age, and we're both flying. He's happy and fit. If there's a fly in the house, he'll catch it – he's that fit. I keep him very well and feed him at the right times. I walk him every morning. I have to make sure he has water the whole time.

We look after each other. He looks after me and I look after him. I treat him as I treat myself. He's a great dog, the best you could ever meet. If someone came to me and said, 'I'll give you one thousand euro for him,' I wouldn't take it even if I hadn't a shoe on me. I love him that much.

# ACKNOWLEDGEMENTS

The stars of this book are the animal lovers who so graciously and patiently told us their stories. They live in all corners of the country, from Donegal to Wexford, from Kerry to Antrim, and most counties in between. We cannot thank them enough for their kindness.

We are grateful to a number of contributors who identified further useful contacts and stories. They include Tom Curran, Josephine Curran, John Mc Grath, John Kennedy, Paud Curran, Sheila Kennedy, Jonathan, Jeremiah and Pat Kennedy.

Other individuals who are not in the book but who were most helpful include John Daly, Declan Terry, Shaun Gallagher, Ann Kelliher, Tom Donovan, Martin Hearne, Kathleen O'Connor, Mike Hackett, Joanna McCarthy, David Finn, Saoirse Curran and Patricia Cullen. Our appreciation also extends to Helen Keane and to Hilary McGouran, Managing Editor, RTÉ TV News.

Two people deserving special mention are Linda Monahan, from Typeform, for her excellent work in designing the cover; also Typeform's Barbara Ryan for laying out the text. Others include Shea Tomkins of *Ireland's Own*, Erin Hutcheon of the *Derry Journal*, Noel Cronin and Rose Curtin of CRY 104FM, and Weeshie Fogarty of Radio Kerry. The *Belfast Telegraph* was supportive, as always.

On the book front, anyone who wants an amusing insight to donkeys should read *M'asal Beag Dubh*, or *My Little Black*

*Donkey*, by Pádraic Ó Conaire, which was referred to in the Helpful Companions chapter. The text can be difficult to find, although some public libraries keep copies.

We would like to specifically thank a young and talented musician, Joseph Ryan, who is based in London and whose conversation with us while we were writing this book was both inspiring and encouraging. He brought light into our lives. To Professor Con Timon, our appreciation also. His medical interventions kept this show on the road.

Our final words of gratitude are reserved for the animals whose stories we profiled. They were all wonderful creatures, full of innocence and fun, enhancing their owners' lives and filling their hearts with joy. Without them, there would have been no *Animal Crackers*.

# GOING HOME

## IRISH STORIES FROM THE EDGE OF DEATH

### Colm Keane

Going Home contains the most comprehensive insights ever provided by Irish people into what happens when we die.

Many of those interviewed have clinically died – some after heart attacks, others after long illnesses or accidents. They have returned to claim – 'There is life after death!'

Most have travelled through dark tunnels and entered intensely bright lights. Some have been greeted by dead relatives and met a superior being. All have floated outside their bodies and watched themselves down below.

Those left behind describe visions of relatives who passed away. The book also acquaints us with the latest scientific research.

Award-winning journalist Colm Keane has spoken to people from all corners of Ireland and recounts their stories.

Based on years of research, Going Home provides us with the most riveting insight we may ever get into where we go after death.

### Reviews of *Going Home*

'Fascinating' *Irish Daily Mail*
'Intriguing' *Sunday World*
'A beautiful, satisfying, comforting book' *Radio Kerry*

# THE DISTANT SHORE

## MORE IRISH STORIES FROM THE EDGE OF DEATH

### Colm Keane

The Distant Shore is packed with a wealth of new Irish stories about life after death.

Extraordinary accounts of what takes place when we die are featured throughout. Reunions with deceased relatives and friends, and encounters with a 'superior being', are included.

Visions of dead family members are vividly described. The book also examines astonishing premonitions of future events.

This compilation was inspired by the huge response to Colm Keane's number one bestseller Going Home – a groundbreaking book that remained a top seller for six months.

Containing new material and insights, The Distant Shore is indispensable reading for those who want to know what happens when we pass away.

### Reviews of *The Distant Shore*

'Amazing new stories' *Irish Independent*

'Terrific, wonderful read' *Cork 103 FM*

'A source of genuine comfort to anyone who has suffered a bereavement' *Western People*

# FOREWARNED

## EXTRAORDINARY IRISH STORIES OF PREMONITIONS AND DREAMS

### Colm Keane

Did you ever have a feeling that something bad was going to happen? Perhaps you dreamt of a future event? Maybe you had a 'gut feeling' that an illness, death, car crash or some other incident was about to occur?

Most Irish people, at various stages of their lives, have experienced a forewarning of the future. It may reveal itself as a sense of unease. Alternatively, it may be more intense and involve a terrifying foreboding. Perhaps it brings good news.

Forewarned is the first Irish enquiry into this intriguing phenomenon. Crammed with fascinating stories, the book also presents the latest scientific evidence proving that the future is closer to our minds than we think.

Reviews of *Forewarned*

'Amazing stories' *Belfast Telegraph*

'Authenticity of experience is written all over these reports' *Irish Catholic*

'A fascinating read' *Soul & Spirit*

# WE'LL MEET AGAIN

## IRISH DEATHBED VISIONS
## WHO YOU MEET WHEN YOU DIE

### Colm Keane

We do not die alone. That's the remarkable conclusion of this extraordinary book examining deathbed visions.

Parents, children, brothers, sisters and close friends who have already died are among those who return to us as we pass away. Religious figures appear to others, while more see visions of beautiful landscapes.

Riveting case histories are featured, along with numerous stories from those left behind who describe after-death visitations and many other strange occurrences. The latest scientific evidence is discussed.

*We'll Meet Again,* written by award-winning journalist Colm Keane, is one of the most challenging books ever compiled on this intriguing theme.

Reviews of *We'll Meet Again*

'A total page-turner' *Cork 103 FM*
'Packed with riveting case histories' *LMFM Radio*
'A fascinating book' *Limerick's Live 95FM*

If you wish to contact us about an animal or pet story for future publication purposes, we can be reached at: capelislandpress@hotmail.com or Capel Island Press, Baile na nGall, Ring, Dungarvan, County Waterford.